Stan Getz

NOBODY ELSE BUT ME

Stan Getz

NOBODY ELSE BUT ME

DAVE GELLY

Stan Getz
NOBODY ELSE BUT ME

DAVE GELLY

A BACKBEAT BOOK
First edition 2002
Published by Backbeat Books
600 Harrison Street,
San Francisco, CA94107
www.backbeatbooks.com

An imprint of The Music Player Network United
Entertainment Media Inc.

Published for Backbeat Books by Outline Press Ltd,
115J Cleveland Street, London W1T 6PU, England.
www.backbeatuk.com

ISBN 0-87930-729-3

Art Director: Nigel Osborne
Design: Paul Cooper
Editorial Director: Tony Bacon
Editor: Paul Quinn
Production: Phil Richardson

Printed by Colorprint (Hong Kong)

02 03 04 04 06 5 4 3 2 1

Contents

Introduction

Whenever Stan Getz stepped out onto the stage and began to play, the listener's first reaction was one of disbelief. No matter how well prepared you were, you never expected the sound to be quite as beautiful as it was. It's said that Heifetz produced the same effect in person. Duke Ellington's orchestra certainly did, and so did Frank Sinatra. In Getz's case, the magic worked regardless of where he was playing – in a small jazz club or a vast concert hall. It was as though he carried his own acoustics around with him. Many, if not most, jazz saxophonists close their eyes when playing, but Getz stared straight ahead. There was something quite unnerving about that piercing, blue-eyed gaze.

Both of these things, the in-person sound and the stare, are lost to us forever. Eventually there will be no one left who remembers them. Fortunately, however, Stan Getz's creative life fell into the second half of the 20th century, the age of reliable sound recording. Recorded music is never quite as good as live music, but it is infinitely preferable to the silence of the grave, which was the fate of performed music in earlier times. Getz's genius is enshrined in his records. They represent the art he practised on most days of his adult existence and they tell the story of his musical mind, his inner life. As we shall see, the steadfast purity of this inner life was sometimes wildly at odds with the chaos and squalor that beset his outer life.

Jazz musicians, even great ones, rarely become truly popular figures. Names like Charlie Parker, Dizzy Gillespie or John Coltrane may register vaguely with the general public, but that's usually as far as it goes. Only a select few have managed to break through to the next level of recognition. Their records sell in respectable quantities and they fill large concert halls. Erroll Garner was one of these, so was the Dave Brubeck Quartet, so was the Count Basie Orchestra – and so was Stan Getz. The initial impetus may have come from an unexpected hit number (Garner's 'Misty', Brubeck's 'Take Five', Basie's 'April In Paris', Getz's 'Desafinado'), but their music was engaging enough to hold onto the audience after the initial fuss had died down. They all have one simple quality in common, namely that they are superficially pleasant to listen to. You don't have to know anything about jazz, or be able to follow the logic of an improvised solo, or even know the names of the instruments, to like the noise they make. In this respect, Getz's mellifluous tone was his fortune.

At the time of his death, on June 6th 1991, several obituaries hailed Getz as having been a "pioneer" who "changed the face of jazz". This is a form of praise commonly applied in jazz, but in Getz's case it is not really true. In two respects he influenced developments – in disseminating Lester Young's approach to the tenor saxophone, and in popularising the bossa nova as a jazz genre – but essentially he was a unique and highly personal artist who spoke for nobody but himself. The real change took place within his own playing, which grew and deepened throughout his life, sometimes even reaching beyond the confines of jazz itself. But unlike, say, Miles Davis, whose stylistic mutations were so sudden and so radical as to render his later playing virtually unrecognisable as the work of the same person, Getz remained characteristically Getz from beginning to end.

Dave Gelly, London, July 2002

CHAPTER 1

Another Time
Another Place

"Hawkins was king, until he met those crazy Kansas City tenor men."

PIANIST MARY LOU WILLIAMS ON THE NEW APPROACH TO SAXOPHONE PLAYING AS LED BY LESTER YOUNG

Stan Getz played the saxophone, the tenor saxophone, although 'playing' is too bland a word to describe the close and intimate bond between man and instrument. The saxophone was as much a part of him as his own voice. Yet if he had been born in another era, or into another culture, they would never have met. If the pogroms of 1903 had not driven his grandparents from the Ukraine in the first place, he might have played the bassoon in a symphony orchestra, or the clarinet in an itinerant band, performing at peasant weddings.

Quite possibly he would have died in the upheavals and famines of the early Soviet period, or in the conflict we call World War Two and Russians call the Great Patriotic War. If he had not been brought up poor, in New York City, during the 1930s, his life, and hence his music, would have been very different. In any event, the musical phenomenon we know as 'Stan Getz' would never have existed.

Every artist, however original and distinctive, belongs to a place and a moment in history. These determine the idiom in which he works and the materials available to him. In Getz's case the idiom was

A teenage Stan Getz in the mid 1940s

jazz, an American music, and the medium was the saxophone, an obscure French invention of the mid-19th century which eventually found a home in American popular entertainment. In 1927, the year of his birth, the first generation of jazz saxophonists was just beginning to emerge, although their early efforts were not promising. There were thousands of saxophone players in the dance bands of dance-crazy 1920s America, but when one of them stood up to take a solo (or 'hot chorus') the result, almost inevitably, was a kind of aimless hooting. The problem lay in the lack of clear stylistic models. Trumpeters could draw inspiration from the blazing confidence of the young Louis Armstrong, clarinettists could emulate the filigree perfection of Jimmie Noone or the soulfulness of Leon Ropollo, trombonists had Kid Ory or George Brunis. All these style-setters were among the first wave of New Orleans musicians to take jazz to the wider world. But the saxophone scarcely figured at all in New Orleans music, so an approach to it had to be invented from scratch.

As far as the tenor saxophone is concerned, this feat was accomplished by Coleman Hawkins. Born in St Joseph, Missouri in 1904, Hawkins was playing professionally with Mamie Smith's Jazz Hounds at the age of 17. In 1924 he joined Fletcher Henderson's orchestra and, by playing Henderson's records in chronological order, it's quite possible to trace the progress of Hawkins's epic struggle to develop a consistent and expressive tenor style. He finally managed it towards the end of 1929, in two numbers recorded with a novelty band called the Mound City Blues Blowers: 'Hello, Lola!' and 'If I Could Be With You One Hour Tonight'. The first of these is a lively, high-spirited piece and the second a romantic ballad. Hawkins tackles both with poise, authority and a broad, focused tone which no other tenor saxophonist had ever come within miles of achieving. From that moment, it was accepted that the sound of the tenor was the sound of Coleman Hawkins. His recording of 'Body And Soul', made ten years later, is one of the great, undisputed classics of jazz.

The saxophone, already a fixture in dance bands, made great strides as a jazz instrument throughout the 1930s. The example of Hawkins on tenor, of Benny Carter and Johnny Hodges on alto, and of their innumerable followers, quickly made itself felt. By the beginning of the decade, the American dance orchestra had finally settled into its standard shape of brass, saxophone and rhythm sections. When the swing era took off, in the mid-Thirties, this was already the universal format, used by bands of all styles, from Benny Goodman, the "King of Swing", to Guy Lombardo and his self-styled "sweetest music this side of heaven". Beneath the top echelon of such big-name bands came layer upon layer of lesser ones, down through 'territory' bands – which toured limited but still quite large areas – to strictly local, part-time outfits.

This whole edifice came into being with phenomenal speed. The rapid spread of swing and the very idea of big-band music was made possible by the development of network radio, the first truly universal medium of entertainment. For the first time, music could be turned on and off like tap water. All you needed was access to a radio set. After that it was free, which meant that even poor people could enjoy it, and there were plenty of those in Depression America. Poor people like Al and Goldie Getz, of Minford Place in the East Bronx, and their two sons, Stanley and Robert. And it didn't matter where you lived, in a penthouse on Riverside Drive or a wooden shack in Dogpatch, Tennessee, the voices of Bing Crosby or Ruth Etting or Whispering Jack Smith were as familiar to you as those of your own family, and the music of bands provided the soundtrack to everyday life.

Radio blurred the cultural diversity of America, but did not by any means obliterate it. Local variations on the standard big-band style soon began to appear. In Oklahoma and Texas, for example, brass and saxophones were joined by fiddles and steel guitars to create the joyful hybrid called Western Swing. In the great 'blues triangle', with its northern apex at Kansas City and and southern base-points in Georgia to the east and Texas to the west, black bands had already begun developing a distinctive style of their own. The saxophonist Garvin Bushell, whose immensely long career took in playing with Mamie Smith's Jazz Hounds at one end and John Coltrane at the other, recalled travelling through the area in the late 1920s. "Most bands included a saxophone," he said. "They just played the blues, one after another, at different tempos."[1] Among those south-western bands might have been the Blue Devils, with their young pianist Bill Basie, and one of those saxophonists, endlessly playing the blues, could well have been the even more youthful Lester Young.

LESTER LEAPS IN

In the fullness of time, Basie came to lead his own band. It was resident at the Reno Club in Kansas City and consisted of only nine players, but it had a reputation for powerful swing and exciting soloists, notably the tenor saxophone of Lester Young. Radio was the means by which Basie's band came to the notice of John Hammond, jazz promoter and record producer, in 1936. Idly searching for music on his car radio late one night in a Chicago parking lot, he came across Basie, broadcasting live from the Reno Club, and was completely captivated by what he heard. Although another recording director got to Basie first and signed up the band, now enlarged to 14 pieces, Hammond quickly recorded a quintet drawn from its members, in October 1936. One of those five was Lester Young. He was 27 years old and it was the first time he had been inside a recording studio.

Lester Young had been a nomad for most of his life, and a musician from the age of ten. That was when he began playing with the band led by his father, Willis Young, which travelled around, entertaining at carnivals and tent-shows. He began as a drummer but soon switched to the saxophone. He left the family band in 1927, in Salina, Kansas, unwilling to endure what he knew would be a humiliating tour through the Deep South, and spent the next few years drifting from band to band. As he did so, he acquired a reputation for musical inventiveness and an approach to the instrument which was all his own. By the time he joined Basie, in 1934, Lester already had a considerable underground reputation among musicians. He had even eclipsed Hawkins at a furiously competitive jam session, much to the delight of his highly partisan Kansas City supporters. ("Yes, Hawkins was king, until he met those crazy Kansas City tenor men," crowed the pianist Mary Lou Williams.)[2]

But Kansas City, 'KC', represented a little world of its own. Ruled with ruthless efficiency by a gangster-politician, Tom Pendergast, it boomed throughout the 1930s as though the Depression didn't exist. It was said that there was no such thing as an unemployed musician in KC. But it was remote from media centres, especially New York, where the recording industry and the big radio networks were based. The rest of the country knew virtually nothing about the music being played in Kansas City and the south-west. Hammond, in Chicago, had only caught Basie broadcasting from a local KC station by a fluke.

And so it was that Lester Young's first recording, released in early 1937, arrived like a despatch from outer space. In two pieces, each less than three minutes long, he managed to upset every tenet established by Hawkins for the tenor saxophone in jazz. Hawkins was a heavyweight. His tone was broad, with a hard cutting edge. He ploughed through his improvisations like a battleship through heavy seas, dismantling popular tunes, brushing aside the simple harmonies provided by their composers and creating in their place a complex structure full of chromatic substitutions and passing chords. Like the man himself, it was vastly impressive and almost intimidating in its self-assurance.

Lester Young, by contrast, played with a light, floating tone and in place of force he employed wit. Far from seeking harmonic complexity, he seemed intent on using the simplest notes possible, but the simplicity was teasing and deceptive. He could bounce around on just two notes like a child hopping from one foot to another, but the pattern thus created would be maddeningly elusive. Those first two recorded numbers, 'Lady Be Good' and 'Shoe Shine Boy', are full of such moments. He was a shy, dreamy, sweet-natured young man. In this, too, he was the exact opposite of Hawkins.

So now there were two ways of playing the tenor saxophone. Lester Young's debut met with a guarded reception at first. Generally speaking, established musicians rejected his playing out of hand. As far as they were concerned this wasn't the way to do it. But over the next few years, as Basie's band became established – with Lester as one of its star soloists – the antagonism gradually melted away, and he also began to attract a new following among very young fans. By the time Lester left Basie, in December 1940, Stan Getz was 13 years old and had just acquired his first saxophone.

Music of all kinds poured from the radio in a vast, impartial flow, and there is no way of knowing exactly what young Stanley Getz heard, or what particularly caught his ear. Taking tenor saxophonists in big bands alone, in late 1940 he could have heard, among others: Lester Young with Count Basie, Eddie Miller with Bob Crosby, Ben Webster with Duke Ellington, Chu Berry with Cab Calloway, Budd Johnson with Earl Hines, Tex Beneke with Glenn Miller, Georgie Auld with Benny Goodman and Dick Wilson with Andy Kirk's Clouds Of Joy. There is no more absorbent material in the universe than the mind of a teenage boy with an obsession, so it's likely that he heard, and could recognise, all of them.

What he could not know was that, down in the south-west, touring out of Kansas City, was a band led by pianist Jay McShann, containing a 20-year-old alto saxophonist called Charlie Parker. In this same year, Parker met up for the first time with the 23-year-old Dizzy Gillespie, then playing in Cab Calloway's trumpet section. These two were soon to become leaders of the bebop movement, which would bring about profound changes to the sound and spirit of jazz in the coming few years.

This was the jazz world that the proud new owner of an ancient and somewhat decrepit saxophone would soon be entering.

CHAPTER 2

A Tuxedo And
A Toothbrush

"I'd only been playing two years and I stank, really... but I sat in with the band and I got the job."

STAN GETZ, ON JOINING JACK
TEAGARDEN'S BIG-BAND

According to Stan Getz's own version of events, he might have been born an Englishman – although the odds were heavily stacked against his being born at all. Both his sets of grandparents, the Gayetskis and the Yampolskys, walked and begged lifts from Kiev to the west in 1903. After stopping briefly in Paris, the Gayestskis settled in Whitechapel, in the East End of London, where Stan's grandfather, Haris Gayetski, started a small tailoring business. This was where Stan's father, Al, was born.

Other members of the family had crossed to the United States and were doing quite well in Philadelphia. They urged Haris to join them, and he began saving up to buy steerage tickets for the maiden voyage of the Titanic in 1912. Luckily, he could not get the cash together in time and was forced to postpone the trip. The London Gayetskis finally sailed for New York in 1914, aboard the Lusitania. Once again, Haris Gayetski was lucky. If he had waited until the following year the family might have perished when the Lusitania was sunk by the Imperial German Navy in May 1915.

In Stan Kenton's sax section: Getz (centre) with Eddie Meyers and Bob Gioga, Kenton on right.

Stan Getz NOBODY ELSE BUT ME

On arrival in the US, the Gayetskis became Getzes and settled in Philadelphia. This is where Stan was born, on 2nd February 1927, the first-born son and the first grandchild for either side of the family. To say he was doted on, especially by his mother Goldie, would be a serious understatement. Although Al, his father, seemed incapable of rising above the level of casual work in the printing industry, young Stan was indulged and pampered throughout his childhood. It might repay some academic researcher one day to make a study of the number of great jazz musicians who were petted and spoiled by their mothers – Stan Getz, Charlie Parker and Miles Davis come most immediately to mind. The family lived in the Meadows, a poor district of Philadelphia which, like most poor districts of the time, seems to have produced its fair share of musicians and entertainers. One of these, the pianist and singer Buddy Greco, speaking off the top of his head about his Philadelphia contemporaries, listed Al Martino, Frankie Avalon, Fabian, and one Freddie Cocozza, "a tough kid who changed his name to Mario Lanza".[1] He also named Stan Getz, although the Getz family left Philadelphia for the Bronx when Stan was six.

In later life, Getz was fond of recounting his introduction to musical performance, at the age of about ten, and told the story many times. It began with a visit to his school by a vaudeville group, Borrah Minevich & His Harmonica Rascals. The next day, as he recalled, "I was sitting on the stoop and this lady came by. She was from the Borrah Minevich Junior Harmonica Rascals, and she asked me if I wanted to buy a harmonica and a booklet to learn how to play it. So my mother gave me the 50 cents and I proceeded, during that summer, to learn how to play 'Silent Night' and 'I'm A Old Cowhand From The Rio Grande'. And at the end of the summer, in the school auditorium, they gathered all the children who were doing creative things to keep them out of trouble – which is what it was for. Some of the wealthier parents, their children were playing piano, violin, things like that. I got up on stage, with a pair of new white duck pants that my mother bought for the occasion, and I proceeded to swing right into 'Silent Night' with all my heart and soul. And I was so nervous that I started to wet my new duck pants. But I didn't stop playing, and the grey spot on my pants kept getting bigger and bigger. And all the insensitive mothers in the audience laughed and the ones who felt for me were very sad about it. And my mother felt so sorry for me, too. And that was my introduction to music."[2]

Undeterred by this dampening experience, he still felt the urge to play a musical instrument of some kind. His next opportunity came at junior high school, when he was 12. The physical training instructor, who was also the school bandmaster, called the class together one day.

"He said, 'You, Getz – come with me!' He took me upstairs to the tower of the school, which was the orchestra rehearsal hall, and he said, 'This is a bass fiddle. We're playing a concert in the school auditorium in two weeks and I have no one to play the bass part of the 'Minuet' from Mozart's E-flat Symphony. You are elected.' And he proceeded to show me how to bow the bass. Now when I was a child, I bit my fingernails, and from pressing into the fingerboard the blood would run down the instrument. That's how I stopped biting my nails.

"He said, 'Take it home and practise it.' So I took it home, through the streets, and all the kids were shouting, 'Hey, Getz, whaddya doin' with that thing? Come on, let's play stickball,' and so forth. And I marched it up the six flights to our little apartment … my mother opened the door and she leaned against the door with her arms folded, looked at me and looked at the bass for a long time. Finally she said, 'There's room in here for only one of you. Which one's it gonna be?'"[3]

SIXTH SENSE

Mrs Getz finally relented and Stan played bass in the school orchestra for a while. Although he had no particular liking for the instrument, the experience did reveal something about him which no-one had hitherto suspected, namely that he possessed the gift of perfect pitch. This attribute, sometimes called 'absolute pitch', occurs in about one in ten thousand of the population of the Western world[4]. The Harvard Dictionary Of Music defines it as "the ability to identify immediately a musical sound by name or to sing any tone at will". It is really a special kind of memory and seems to be related to the language-learning process in infancy. It is often, but by no means always, passed down in families, and people sometimes don't even know they have it. They just assume everybody hears that way. Perfect pitch can sometimes be a nuisance, to musicians playing with out-of-tune pianos, for example, but mostly it amounts to a valuable sixth sense. It's not to be confused with a 'good ear', a well-developed sense of relative pitch, which is essential for any musician.

What the young Stan Getz really craved was an instrument on which he could play melodies. The saxophone particularly appealed to him, although the chances of getting hold of one seemed remote.

"My father … he didn't tell me this at the time, but he saved his lunch money, didn't have any lunch for a year, and he bought me this little silver sax, alto saxophone, that was actually a mouldy green colour. And that's how I started to play saxophone."[5]

This was in the month of his 13th birthday, February 1940, and he immediately began to take regular lessons from a local teacher, Bill Scheiner, at 25 cents a time. Scheiner had several saxophones which he let his pupils try out. Stan was instantly captivated by the tenor – larger than the alto and pitched in B-flat – and set his heart on somehow getting one of his own some day. Now that he had an instrument and a proper teacher it was obvious that music was to be Stanley Getz's life. To complement his gift of perfect pitch, he had a natural affinity not only with the saxophone but apparently with any woodwind instrument. The clarinet gave him no trouble, and neither did the bassoon. In fact, the speed with which he mastered the notoriously wayward bassoon indicates just what a prodigy he was.

He took it up in order to get into his school's main orchestra. James Monroe High boasted a full-sized symphony orchestra and Getz, now aged 14, realised that he needed the challenge of playing at the highest standard. The answer was to get into the orchestra – so when he learned that the second bassoon desk was about to become vacant he borrowed a school instrument, having first extracted the deposit from his mother, took it home and practised it over the summer vacation.

When school reassembled he took an audition and passed easily. Within a year he had progressed to the All-City High School Orchestra and was taking lessons from Simon Kovar, first bassoonist with the New York Philharmonic.

Stan Getz NOBODY ELSE BUT ME

At the same time, he had begun playing his little mouldy-green alto saxophone at local functions – socials, weddings, bar mitzvahs – for around three dollars a night. This was quite good money in 1941, especially for a 14-year-old, and his contribution made an appreciable difference to the family finances. He was also saving up furiously to buy a tenor saxophone. Judging by occasional comments he made in later life, and indeed his actions when he was on the fringes of the big time, Getz seems to have felt the weight of family responsibilities at a very tender age. In the world of his childhood, any glimmering of talent represented a potential escape route from the cycle of poverty. The pressure to succeed by capitalising on his gift must have been relentless, and it probably accounts for what happened next.

Stan eventually acquired a tenor saxophone and found himself in increasing demand. At 15, he had the instrumental technique of a professional, could sight-read anything put in front of him, play virtually any tune by ear after hearing it a couple of times, imitate the styles of well-known players and improvise simple solos. In short, he was in possession of the jobbing musician's complete kit, which made him a highly marketable commodity. It was only a matter of time before an attractive proposition came his way, and it arrived towards the end of 1942. Dick 'Stinky' Rogers, then leading one of the bands at Roseland Ballroom in Manhattan, offered him a regular job at $35 a week. This was more than his father could earn, even when he was in work. On the other hand, there was the undeniable fact that Stan had not yet reached school-leaving age. But the $35 a week won, and Stan began work at Roseland in December.

This was a fully professional engagement, which meant that all the musicians had to be union members. The wheels were put in motion and, on 14th January 1943, Stanley Getz was admitted into Local 802 of the American Federation of Musicians. Almost simultaneously, the Board of Education's truancy officer caught up with him. He was unceremoniously sacked and returned to school, with his union card in his pocket and mutiny in his heart. Within a matter of days he was on the lookout for another job.

"I went down to a rehearsal in Manhattan with a friend of mine who was playing with Jack Teagarden's orchestra. There was a war on, and all the good musicians were drafted. The only ones you could get were either 4F [medically unfit], too young or too old – and I was too young. The tenor saxophone player didn't show up for rehearsal that day, so Teagarden said to my friend, who was playing alto saxophone in the band, 'Hey, Gate... uh... you got any pals around here that play the tenor saxophone?'" (Getz, who was a very good mimic, could reproduce Teagarden's Texas drawl with uncanny accuracy.) "And he said, 'Why, my friend sitting right there is a superb tenor saxophone player.' I'd only been playing two years and I stank, really... but I sat in with the band and I got the job. And Teagarden said, 'We're leaving for Boston in the morning. I wancha get a tuxedo, a spare white shirt and your toothbrush, and be at Penn Station at ten o'clock in the morning'.

"Here was a chance to earn $70 a week and support my whole family – send 40 home, live on 30 and travel. Now, that particular weekend, my mother was visiting her family in Philadelphia. If she'd been home she wouldn't have allowed it, money or no money. She wanted me to have my schooling, and she also knew that the Director of Music at my high-school had promised me a four-year full scholarship to Juilliard – and so instead of being a famous saxophone player now I might have been a very mediocre symphony composer."[6] It's more likely he would have become a successful orchestral bassoonist, but that was how he liked to tell the story.

BIG TEA

Jack Teagarden, often known as 'Big Tea', is an important figure in the history of jazz. He was born in 1905, and in some respects he did for the trombone what Coleman Hawkins did for the tenor saxophone. He rescued it from the raucous, clownish role to which early jazz bands often consigned it and gave it a lyrical voice. He also gave it unprecedented mobility. While his contemporaries plodded earnestly along, Teagarden would scamper around like a puppy on the loose. And he did all this using only the first three of the seven slide positions: he'd begun playing as a child, when his arm was too short to reach any further, and evolved a personal technique – managing to get the full range of notes from just those three positions – which worked so well that he never bothered to change it.

From the moment of his first appearance, as a teenager in Peck Kelly's band, Teagarden was recognised as a master. He starred with Ben Pollack for five years and in 1933 joined Paul Whiteman's hugely popular show-band as featured trombonist and singer. He was a most engaging vocalist, so laid-back that he seemed to be delivering the song from the depths of a rocking chair, and his tenure with Whiteman made him a popular radio star. During the 1930s Teagarden also played literally hundreds of freelance recording sessions, with bands such as the Charleston Chasers and the Venuti-Lang All-Stars, many of which produced classic performances.

Leaving Whiteman in 1938, Teagarden set about forming his own big-band. This is what successful sidemen did and it was expected of him. Although Jack Teagarden & His Orchestra was a late entry in a crowded field, it did quite well at first. In 1941 the band was featured, and Teagarden had a speaking-and-singing part, in the movie Birth Of The Blues, starring Bing Crosby and Mary Martin. One of the most delightful and witty of all Hollywood production numbers is 'The Waiter And The Porter And The Upstairs Maid' in this film, featuring the three of them.

By 1943, however, Teagarden was in trouble. The war not only meant that experienced musicians between the ages of 21 and 35 were being drafted into the armed forces, it also made long-distance touring by road next to impossible. There was a government ban on the use of buses for non-essential purposes and private cars were virtually ruled out because the rubber shortage meant tyres were unobtainable. That's why the young Getz was told to report to Pennsylvania railway station for that first trip to Boston.

There was a huge demand for entertainment, including dancing to bands, but the bands could not move around the country to satisfy it. And to help matters along, the American Federation of Musicians (AFM) had just called an indefinite strike against the record industry. All this was bad enough, but Teagarden was not the man to battle his way through such difficulties. Everyone said the same thing about him: he was a brilliant musician, a charismatic entertainer, a lovely man – but no bandleader. Successful bandleaders were hard men, like Tommy Dorsey, or cold fish, like Benny Goodman, or sharp trend-spotters, like Harry James. There were a few recognisable humans among them, like Count Basie and

Stan Getz NOBODY ELSE BUT ME

Woody Herman, but they were exceptions. Furthermore, Teagarden was a drinker of epic proportions. The amount of whisky he consumed in the average day should have finished him off years ago, but his tolerance of alcohol was phenomenal. He was never quite sober, but rarely totally incapable.

With his mother away from home, and his father easily persuaded by the prospect of the $70 a week salary, Stan left for Boston the following morning. He was still under age, and the authorities again caught up with him a few weeks later, in St Louis. This time, though, it was agreed he could stay with the band, if Teagarden would undertake to become his legal guardian and ensure he did some schoolwork. The fact that Teagarden's was a household name may have carried weight with the education bureaucrats and Stan's parents. Whatever the case, papers were signed and Stan Getz was launched on his career, albeit aboard a somewhat leaky vessel, doubling on tenor and baritone saxophones.

Anyone observing the Getz-Teagarden relationship during those days might have had trouble deciding on who was supposed to be taking care of whom. Teagarden was endlessly enthusiastic and patient when it came to discussing points of musical theory and technique or tricks of stagecraft, and was genuinely delighted to have a bright and receptive young pupil like Stan. On the other hand, when Tea finally nodded off late at night it was Stan's job to put him to bed, and get him up again in the morning with the aid of an array of potions and pick-me-ups.

FIRST STEPS IN THE SPOTLIGHT

For the remainder of 1943, the 15 players of the Teagarden orchestra, plus vocalist Phyllis Lane, shuttled around the US, wherever the booking agency sent them. Like most bands at the time, the bulk of their work was dedicated to the war effort, and paid for by the government, which also arranged transport. They made no records, because of the AFM strike, but they did record several live shows for the Armed Forces Radio Service (AFRS) series *Spotlight Bands*. In August they made one in Wichita Falls, Texas, in September at Barksdale Field, Louisiana, and in November at Blyth Air Force Base, California. There is one brief moment in the Barksdale recording which may, just possibly, be Stan Getz's first recorded utterance – a tantalising four bars in 'Night And Day'. It is gawky, uncertain and slightly rushed – exactly what one would expect from a 16-year-old.

After Blyth, the whole show ground to a halt because Teagarden became ill. Fortunately for him his home was in Los Angeles, so he folded the band and retired to bed for a while. A few weeks later, feeling a little better, he formed a temporary band out of local musicians and any of his old crew who were still around, including Stan. Teagarden did not yet feel up to the rigors of touring and restricted himself to AFRS broadcasts, a few short films and the odd local gig. Thus Stan's membership of the Teagarden orchestra petered out, and their formal connection ended in February 1944, with Stan's 17th birthday.

For the rest of his life, Stan Getz thought of Jack Teagarden with enormous affection. Although their relationship had started out as a legal fiction, he had grown to regard Jack almost as a real father, someone who taught him things he wanted to know, who encouraged him, gave him the occasional solo spot and took pleasure in his growing abilities. But this was not the only legacy of Stan's time with Big Tea.

He'd joined as a talented and determined 16-year-old boy. He left at 17, still talented and determined, but now putting away a bottle of bourbon every single day.

Stan was enchanted by southern California and resolved to make it his home. Having sat out the 90-day residence qualification decreed by the AFM, he worked with a number of local bands, including the sextet which acted as permanent relief band at the Hollywood Palladium, reputed to be the biggest and smartest ballroom in the country. At this point he sent for his parents, enclosing railroad tickets for them and his brother, Robert, promising that their hard times were over. And they came. One wonders how many families would have abandoned everything familiar to them and travelled 3000 miles to an uncertain future at the behest of a 17-year-old boy, no matter how glittering his prospects. As it turned out, the parents never could get used to LA and returned to New York a few years later.

The wartime draft was still severely affecting the band business and in the spring of 1944 Stan Kenton's orchestra lost both its tenor saxophonists. The replacements were Dave Matthews and Stan Getz, on first and second tenors respectively, and the salary was $125 a week. Government controls on wage increases just did not work in the band business, with musicians constantly changing jobs and bandleaders desperate for their services.

Although a comparatively new bandleader, Kenton was not struggling as Teagarden had been. In the first place, his was the resident band on Bob Hope's NBC radio show, which attracted an audience of around 20 million listeners a week. Each show came from a different army or navy base and, since Hope was a big star, the entire company travelled courtesy of the US government in a converted B17 bomber. Often the plane would make several stops at isolated military posts en route. Sets and instruments would be unloaded for Hope and the company to give a show, then everything was dismantled and they took off again. From time to time Hope returned to Hollywood to attend to his movie career. That's when Kenton could settle down for several weeks at the Palladium, where his band was a big favourite. He had a recording contract with a new and dynamic label, Capitol Records, whose base was also in Hollywood.

It was a very good deal all round, and Kenton was exactly the man to take advantage of it. He had a talent for publicity, gave an impressive interview, worked tirelessly and made the most of every opportunity. He took the occasional drink, but nobody could recall seeing him even slightly drunk. In short, he was the precise opposite of Big Tea in all respects. This contrast also extended to their music. Teagarden's was warm, mellow, lyrical and deeply tinged with the accents of the blues. Kenton, on the other hand, sought to incorporate the harmonies and textures of modern classical music, especially its more ornate and melodramatic aspects. To this end he gradually increased the size of his brass section to ten and wrote or commissioned arrangements guaranteed to lash audiences into a state of fevered excitement. The sheer volume of the thing was enough to numb the senses. At this fairly early stage, the Kenton orchestra was still a dance band, nominally at least, but it was already heading in the direction of the concert hall, which was to be its natural habitat until Kenton's death in 1979.

So far, the young Getz has appeared only in the role of junior sideman: reliable, technically accomplished and a quick learner, but by no means a creative artist in his own right. It is now around May 1944, and this state of affairs is about to change.

CHAPTER 3

Kai's Krazy Kats

"I went up to Stan Kenton and I said to him, 'What do you think of Lester Young's playing?' And he said, 'Not interesting. Too simple.' And that night I gave my notice in."

STAN GETZ ON LEAVING
KENTON'S BAND IN 1945

Stan Kenton's vocalist, Anita O'Day, had a story which she regularly told to interviewers, concerning the young Stan Getz when he was a newcomer in the Kenton band: "This young man came up to me, figuring I knew my way around as I'd been there a few months, and said, 'Would you ask Stan [Kenton] if I could take a solo on any one of the tunes in the book?' And I said, 'Yeah, I'll ask him.' And, you know what it's like, time passed and I didn't ask him.

"So a few days later he comes up to me again and I thought, 'Oh, God, I said I would.' So I went directly to Stan and said, 'The new guy wants to know if he can have a little solo, eight bars or something like that,' and Stan says, 'Yeah, why not? We'll take out number 28 in the book and he can have the first eight of the second chorus.' So I went back to the kid and said, 'OK, when he calls 28, you're on...'

"Well, the band plays the first chorus and the kid's already out there, pulling up and down on his saxophone sling and getting ready. He keeps looking over at me like, hey, it's my turn, you know? ... So it come to the eight and he starts playing it ... but all he played were eight notes, which weren't bad, but for

With Benny Goodman in California, January 1946

a solo you kind of improvise, and he really didn't do anything very much. At the end he took a little bow and went back to his seat and he's smiling at me. He'd had his first solo and he thought it was terrific. That kid was Stan Getz. That's a beginning, right?"[1]

This cannot have been earlier than May 1944, which is very strange because in the following month Dave Matthews left Kenton and Stan was promoted to first tenor, and his old position went to a newcomer, Emmett Carls. If Anita O'Day's anecdote is to be believed, then Stan Getz's development as a jazz soloist must have been the fastest in history. One thing is certain, he had advanced so far by the winter of 1944 that he was actually receiving on-air credits in the AFRS *One Night Stand* broadcast series: "...and now, winding up in fine style, the tenor saxophone of 17-year-old Stanley Getz and 'Russian Lullaby'."[2]

So, now that we can hear him clearly for the first time, what does he sound like? Well, in 'Russian Lullaby' he sounds exactly like the departed Dave Matthews. It has already been noted that Getz was a talented mimic, and the talent obviously extended to music as well as speech. Indeed, it's all part of the same phenomenon. An ear for accent, timbre and tonal gesture is almost certainly allied to an acute ear for pitch. Although he never did it in public, it is said that Getz could turn out devastating parodies of other saxophonists at the drop of a hat. In this case, he had inherited Matthews's place as first tenor and was making a good professional job of impersonating him.

From the same show comes a duet-feature for the two tenors ("Right now the tenor saxophones of Emmett Carls and Stanley Getz in 'Sergeant's Mess'") in which it is possible to pick Getz out, mainly because he sounds the more like Lester Young of the two. It is a very competent, if unremarkable, performance. Another version, broadcast a week later, finds Getz running through an inventory of Lester Young tonal effects which Carls starts out by trying to emulate but soon gives up.

So why Lester Young? There were two inescapable influences acting on aspiring jazz tenor saxophonists at this time – namely Lester Young and bebop. Jazz historians often lump them together, but they were actually separate. In fact the variety of tenor styles that emerged towards the end of the 1940s was largely the outcome of attempts to reconcile the two.

Lester Young had a kind of delayed-action effect. As we have seen, his arrival in the late 1930s caused consternation among those with established tastes, because he played as though Coleman Hawkins had not existed. Ornate rhetoric was not his style; it was more a matter of nods, winks, sidelong remarks and the odd chuckle, all conjured out of the simplest materials. That is what makes the famous duet passages between him and the young Billie Holiday, recorded during his time with Basie, such perfect miniatures. She was the least rhetorical of singers, conveying a world of meaning with the slightest inflexion, and it is the eloquence of these two minds working in perfect accord which accounts for their devastating charm. It was Billie who named Lester 'Pres' (or 'Prez') short for 'The President', and he dubbed her 'Lady Day'. The names stayed with them both beyond the grave.

All this was happening when Stan Getz and his contemporaries were young teenagers. To them, there was nothing sacrilegious or even odd about Lester Young's playing. Many were drawn to it specifically because it sounded new and modern and had no connection with the sonorities of the past. It was graceful and melodic in its simplicity – contained, undemonstrative. Pres did not reach out to grab your attention like an entertainer; he seemed instead almost to be thinking aloud. This inwardness increased markedly during the period when the Getz generation were starting out as professional musicians.

Lester Young records from late 1943 and 1944 suggest emotional areas which no jazz soloist had ever touched before – ambiguity, irony, self-doubt. But it was all veiled behind an unnerving facade of reticence. The word for it was 'cool'. The archetypal image of Pres at this period is caught in a short film, *Jammin' The Blues*, which depicts a jam session and features him playing a slow blues. For most of his appearance he is pictured alone, in shadow, apparently detached in a world of his own. This was a radical departure from the way jazz musicians were habitually portrayed in films at the time, which was as slightly crazy but happy, fun-loving types (if white), or as eye-rolling drolls (if black).

Jammin' The Blues is a consciously avant-garde piece of work, but it indicates a change in sensibility which was affecting young jazz musicians in big-bands throughout the United States. This was the moment at which Stan Getz began listening avidly to Lester Young's records and emulating his approach to the instrument, as his solos with Kenton reveal.

"I heard Lester Young and he completely turned me around, and I thought, this is simplicity, this is beauty. And one night, after the job, we were all in a restaurant – I think it was in Allentown, Pennsylvania – I went up to Stan Kenton and I said to him, 'What do you think of Lester Young's playing?' And he said, 'Not interesting. Too simple.' And that night I gave my notice in."[3]

FORMING HABITS

Getz had left Teagarden's band with a formidable drink habit and now, in April 1945, he left Kenton with a heroin habit. Whatever the substance, it seemed to have a fatal attraction for Stan Getz. This was a weakness that was to blight his life, cause endless unhappiness to those around him and leave his reputation disfigured by tales of extreme and unpredictable behaviour. Because he was always well paid, he could afford his indulgences and thus keep up an outward appearance of normality. But, as we shall see, it was often a very fragile shell.

After a brief stay with Jimmy Dorsey's band, he spent three months in Hollywood, in a trio at the Swing Club, with pianist Joe Albany and drummer Jimmy Falzone. Albany was among the early adherents of bebop, and had in fact shared an apartment with Charlie Parker the previous year, so it is possible that Getz received his first exposure to the new style from him. In October, Stan had an offer from Benny Goodman and left for Ontario, where Goodman was currently appearing.

In some respects, Goodman and Getz were very similar. They both came from poor Russian-Jewish backgrounds, each had become the principal wage-earner of his family at an early age, they both had the ability to focus on music for long periods to the exclusion of everything else, and they were both phenomenally determined individuals. Getz admired Goodman immensely. "I was in his band at 18," he recalled later, "a fresh kid, and to watch him rehearse a band was something. His ears and musical knowledge, his taste at picking tempos, and choosing guys with good sounds for his bands... wonderful."[4]

Stan Getz NOBODY ELSE BUT ME

Similarly, Goodman liked Getz's playing so much that he even overlooked the kind of teenage horseplay which would have got anyone else fired – although not even Benny Goodman could afford to fire good musicians at that moment. Soon after Getz joined it, the Goodman band settled into a two-month run at the Mosque Theater in Newark, New Jersey, just across the river from Manhattan, and this was when bebop made its first great impact on Stan Getz.

In the closing stages of the war, jazz history was unfolding on New York's 52nd Street, between 5th and 7th Avenues. Here were the basement clubs – the Onyx, Three Deuces, Famous Door, Jimmy Ryan's, Spotlite and many others – where the great jazz artists of half a century could be heard, performing at ease in the intimacy and freedom of small, improvising bands. This in itself must have seemed highly attractive to keen young musicians like Stan Getz. Big-band playing was by its very nature a circumscribed and repetitive job. It entailed playing a single part, in a series of written arrangements, in a programme that remained more or less the same night after night. The need to stretch out, to exercise the musical muscles, to create something, must have become unbearable at times. The answer was the after-hours jam session, as practised in Kansas City and other centres where travelling musicians met. Since before 1940, a new and complex form of jazz had been hatching in Harlem after-hours clubs, such as Minton's Playhouse, on 134th Street, and Clark Monroe's Uptown House on 135th. Among the leading spirits were trumpeter Dizzy Gillespie, pianist Thelonious Monk and drummer Kenny Clarke.

Gillespie was a quite exceptional musician in every respect. Not only was he a naturally gifted player with a phenomenally quick ear, he also had an insatiable curiosity and limitless energy. He listened to modern European composers such as Debussy, Ravel and Stravinsky and was impressed by the fact that they used a much broader harmonic palette than even the most advanced dance-band arranger. He also played the piano and would sit for hours at the keyboard, working out different ways of harmonising a tune. During intervals at the Cotton Club, where he was resident with Cab Calloway's band, he would cajole bassist Milt Hinton into dragging his instrument up to the roof, where they could practise these new ideas undisturbed. After work, the pair of them would head for Minton's and run through familiar jam-session tunes, substituting their new chord sequences, or 'changes', for the regular ones.

In 1942, Jay McShann's band arrived in New York to play at the Savoy Ballroom, and Charlie Parker, McShann's star alto saxophone soloist, at once joined the inner circle at Minton's and Monroe's. He was already thinking along similar lines and formed an instant musical rapport with Gillespie. When McShann's season at the Savoy ended, the band left New York and Parker stayed.

NICE EYES, PRES

The Minton's experimenters were by no means the only ones interested in bringing a new and more sophisticated harmonic slant to jazz. Nat King Cole and his trio, for example, were slipping some extremely advanced harmonies into their performances, but doing it so subtly that the average listener would hardly have noticed, and some big-band arrangers, such as Goodman's Eddie Sauter, were doing the same. Harmonic innovation was in the air.

Changing the harmonic shape of the music meant changing everything else. If playing the old tunes in the swing manner could be likened to cruising along an open country road, then playing them with the new 'changes' was like a high-speed car chase through city streets. The spacious, lyrical phrasing that Louis Armstrong had brought to jazz in the 1920s gave way to cryptic, asymmetric melodic lines, full of sudden swerves and jagged corners. Tempos tended to be either very fast or dead slow, certainly not the comfortable, dance-friendly measures of swing, and this in turn signalled a transformation in the rhythm section. In place of the firm, springy pulse of swing, the piano, bass and drums skimmed unpredictably along, driven by shimmering cymbals and steadied only by the bass.

No one has been able to establish exactly when the name 'bebop' was first applied to this new form of jazz, but it was certainly in use by the time Stan Getz began haunting 52nd Street in late 1945. Dizzy Gillespie had already been named 'New Star' in the previous year's Down Beat magazine's annual awards, an event often taken as marking the moment when bebop began to emerge from underground cult status into full public view, although a few years would have to pass before it could claim any kind of popular following. For the young Stan Getz, this concentrated, close-up exposure to some of the greatest living jazz artists, Charlie Parker in particular, came as a revelation.

Parker, universally known as 'Bird', had arrived by his own route at the same advanced harmonic vocabulary as Dizzy. Indeed, he was so at home with it that it was his natural element. To listen to a Parker solo is to hear a musical mind working on several tasks at once, all at blinding speed. First, there are the notes themselves, then their rhythmic placement, and finally the shape of the whole solo. The notes, as they came flying out, suggested an ever-changing series of harmonic possibilities, and they would be deployed in phrases and accents so tricky that the unwary listener soon lost track of where he was. Bird, however, knew exactly where he was, and could easily drop back into line with a casual turn of phrase. And these details were all part of a broader pattern. Other improvisers thought in phrases and sentences, whereas Parker habitually thought in musical paragraphs. What makes it all the more remarkable is that this astonishing mind, and the equally astonishing technique which served it, was almost always under the influence of drink or drugs – usually both.

Stan Getz's reaction was absolutely typical. "When I first heard Charlie Parker I couldn't believe it," he recalled. "He was ahead of his time. When he played, people said, 'That makes sense, and it's new.' What he created opened up avenues still being explored."[5]

It was Stan's dearest wish to be part of the vibrant 52nd Street scene. What young musician wouldn't? "I wanted to get in with this exciting music, but no-one would let me sit in. No one except Ben, that is." (Ben Webster, former tenor star of Duke Ellington's orchestra, was by then leading a quartet at the Onyx club.) "He knew I was keen, and some nights he'd say, 'All right, kid, get your horn', and I'd blow with the quartet and enjoy that.

"And then one night after I'd played with Ben, there was Lester Young backstage. Pres, you know, had heard me, and you can guess how I felt – I was 18 years old at that time. We met for the first time and I mumbled about what a great pleasure it was.

Stan Getz

"You know Lester spoke in a language all his own? Well, he said to me, 'Nice eyes, Pres. Carry on.' He called me 'Pres'. I'll never forget that."[6]

This meeting probably took place in the early summer of 1946, after Stan had left Goodman, when Pres was in New York for the first time since his release from the US Army. His military service had mostly been spent in the detention barracks at Fort Gordon, Georgia, and the trauma of those eight months stayed with him for the rest of his life. Pres had been discharged on December 15th 1945 and, by a curious coincidence, Stan had made his first small-band jazz recording on the previous day.

By now most big-bands had within their ranks a revolutionary cell of young beboppers, and Goodman's was no exception. In this case it was centred on Stan Getz and trombonist Kai Winding. "[They] carried Charlie Parker records with them on the road and practised playing bebop together in the closet, very secretly. It was like a closed society," recalled baritone saxophonist Danny Bank. "Sometimes Benny would poke his nose in the dressing room and listen to what they were doing; then he'd go, 'Tsk, tsk, tsk' and walk away."[7]

Kai Winding secured a deal with Savoy – a small independent label which was also recording Charlie Parker at the time – to record four titles with a sextet. The band was given the name Kai's Krazy Kats, and its other members were Getz, trumpeter Shorty Rogers (a boyhood pal of Stan's from the East Bronx), pianist Shorty Allen, bassist Iggy Shevack and drummer Shelly Manne. The music itself shows very little evidence of revolutionary backstage activity. In fact, the four numbers ('Sweet Miss', 'Loaded', 'Grab Your Axe, Max' and 'Always') amount mainly to a respectful pastiche of the previous year's Kansas City Seven recordings featuring Lester Young. There are touches of bebop, especially from the two Shorties, Rogers and Allen, but Stan is pure Lester throughout. This is particularly true of his solo entrances, which catch Pres's sidelong manner to perfection. Nice eyes, Pres. Carry on indeed. Lester was later to become quite unsettled by such flattery-by-imitation, and to complain it was invading his creative personality, but who could possibly take exception to this graceful homage from a young admirer?

OPUS DE BOP

The influences of Lester Young on the one hand and Charlie Parker on the other were having an unsettling effect on the young Stan Getz. In the recorded glimpses we get of him at this time he seems to be trying on musical styles like suits of clothes. There are moments on some of Goodman's recorded broadcasts in which the slender, teenaged Getz comes on like a barrel-chested Texas tenor of mature years, and one bizarre solo, on a version of 'Rattle And Roll', dating from February 1946, when he affects a rasping growl all the way through.

With a few exceptions, alto saxophonists simply surrendered to Parker and imitated him as best they could, but this was not possible with the tenor. The only person who ever sounded like Bird on tenor was Bird himself. In some respects, the obvious model was Coleman Hawkins, the only one among the old masters to welcome bebop wholeheartedly and encourage the new generation. He had always been harmonically ahead of his time in any case, and understood what they were seeking to do. But Hawkins's heavy-toned, evenly phrased style was pointing in the wrong direction. All be-boppers revered Lester Young for his sound, his originality and his ineffable cool, but Lester's musical vocabulary was not bebop. When playing with boppers he would pick his way fastidiously through their thickets of advanced changes like a cat, careful not to become entangled. So, throughout the mid-1940s, virtually every tenor player sought to construct his own style by amalgamating Pres and bop.

The one who seems to have impressed Stan Getz most was Dexter Gordon, who was playing with Parker at the Spotlite in late 1945. Six-foot-five tall, confident, debonair, Dexter Keith Gordon was a child of the professional middle class. His father was Duke Ellington's doctor. He played with immense deliberation and calm authority and knew how to wear a suit better than anyone else in the business. He radiated charm and was followed wherever he went by a trail of admirers. Gordon was in the process of developing a simplified bebop style, distinguished by a forceful delivery and shortish, cryptic phrases.

The Dexter Gordon effect had clearly been at work in Stan Getz's playing by July 1946, when he came to record his first quartet session. He is virtually unrecognisable as the tiptoeing Lester Young disciple of a few months earlier. His tone is hard and unyielding, his phrasing brusque, and he plays much more in the gruff lower register of the instrument than ever before or since. In fact, he plays bebop in the Dexter Gordon style just as convincingly as he previously played late-swing in the Lester Young style.

From all points of view, the session of 31st July, again consisting of four numbers ('Opus De Bop', 'Running Water', 'Don't Worry About Me', 'And The Angels Swing'), is undiluted bebop. It would be difficult to imagine a more authentic or uncompromising rhythm section than Hank Jones on piano, Curly Russell on bass and Max Roach on drums. Together they set up not so much a beat as a force-field of nervous energy which drives the music inexorably forward. 'Opus De Bop' is typical. Launched at a headlong 70 bars a minute (which, at four beats per bar, translates to 280 beats per minute) with four bars from Roach, and an eight-bar band introduction, emphasising the beboppers' trademark interval of the flattened fifth, the piece follows the changes of Gershwin's 'I Got Rhythm', suitably embellished with passing chords and substitutions. Hank Jones's theme is really a kind of stylised solo, with neither the repetitions of a standard song nor the insistent riffs of a swing number. This was one of Bird's innovations, and the rest of the performance also follows the Parker pattern closely – a string of solos (with Stan actually sounding rather more fluent than Gordon), four-bar exchanges with drums, eight bars for the bass, a final eight bars of theme, coda – all in two minutes and 29 seconds.

By now Stan had left Benny Goodman, fired for missing a series of shows at New York's Paramount Theater. He had passed briefly through trumpeter Randy Brooks's band and was with Herbie Fields at the Rustic Cabin in Englewood, New Jersey. He was also involved in a serious love affair with 18-year-old vocalist Beverly Byrne, sister of Buddy Stewart, one of the first singers to translate bebop into vocal terms. The couple decided to try their luck together in California. They were married in Los Angeles on November 7th 1946.

Four Brothers

"That band was on everything but roller-skates."

WOODY HERMAN ON HIS
BADLY-BEHAVED SECOND HERD

The war was over, and the celebrations had scarcely died down before the dance-band business began to show signs of incipient collapse. The reasons were complex, and historians are still arguing over them, but the immediate causes certainly included the ratchet of wage inflation, brought on by the wartime shortage of musicians, and a 20 per cent wartime entertainment tax, which the US government had conveniently forgotten to repeal. What's more, people were simply not going out so much. They were settling down, getting married, staying home.

"Finally, in December 1946," writes George T Simon in his monumental volume *The Big Bands*, "almost a dozen years after Benny Goodman had blown the first signs of life into the big-band bubble, that bubble burst with a concerted bang. Inside of just a few weeks, eight of the nation's top bands broke up – Benny Goodman's, Woody Herman's, Harry James's, Tommy Dorsey's, Les Brown's, Jack Teagarden's, Benny Carter's and Ina Ray Hutton's."[1] They would soon be followed by most of the others.

Three cool tenors: Wardell Gray, Zoot Sims, Stan Getz

Stan Getz NOBODY ELSE BUT ME

Whether by accident or design, Stan Getz had made exactly the right move at the right moment. Southern California was the post-war Promised Land, with people pouring in at a phenomenal rate, full of optimism and confidence. As the novelist Walter Mosely put it: "In the late 1940s people came to California, where everything was new and open. Whatever you wanted to do, you could get on and do it, redefine your life."[2] The very fact that big-bands had stopped hiring musicians forced Getz to redefine his own life. It freed him from the constraints and limited contacts that working in a travelling band entailed.

He soon fell in with a group of like-minded musicians and together they shared a rackety but quite lucrative freelance existence around Los Angeles. Among them were saxophonists Zoot Sims and Herbie Steward, pianist Jimmy Rowles, drummer Don Lamond, pianist and arranger Ralph Burns and Stan's old pal, the trumpeter Shorty Rogers, who had been in Herman's band and now found himself at a loose end. "We supported our families by working some dumb jobs," Getz recalled. "We didn't get work playing jazz music, we got work playing rumba bands, Mickey Mouse bands, Dixieland bands – then after work we'd get together for jam sessions."[3]

In fact, the work wasn't all rumbas and Mickey Mouse music by any means. During his first year in Los Angeles, Getz played and broadcast or recorded with temporary studio bands assembled by Goodman, Herman and Neal Hefti, and with saxophonist Vido Musso's dance orchestra, still gamely hanging on at the Meadowbrook Gardens in Culver City. He can be heard playing his only recorded alto saxophone solo on 'Blue Rhythm Blues', by another studio group, the Blue Rhythm Band.

The two surviving numbers from the Musso broadcast in February are the earliest from this period to contain Getz solos, and they reveal that he has finally found his point of stylistic balance between Pres and bop. He sounds utterly confident and is clearly not imitating anyone. The tone is round and slightly hollow, and he has hit upon a characteristic way of articulating his phrases, getting from one note to another, which was to remain one of his trademarks for almost the next decade. The notes tend to come in pairs, the first half-swallowed and the other fully voiced, a curiously ambiguous effect, suggesting both cockiness and vulnerability. At the same time, his delivery is completely poker-faced, expressionless, a study in cool. This is particularly noticeable in the number called 'Gone With Vido', which is a joint feature for Getz and Musso. It would be difficult to find two more diverse approaches to the tenor saxophone – Vido, an excitable player who tended to express himself in a kind of wheezing bellow, and the unnervingly calm young man at his side.

FOUR COOL TENORS

By the summer of 1947, Getz's name had become well-known enough for him to be included in a Just Jazz concert, one of a series of events organised by the jazz disc-jockey and entrepreneur Gene Norman. Like the bigger and more well-known Jazz At The Philharmonic (JATP), these shows catered for a new, post-war generation of dedicated jazz fans who wanted to hear musicians improvising informally, as though playing purely for their own satisfaction. Of course, it never worked out quite like that. The players were all professionals and fully aware that they were performing before an audience, but the success of presentations such as this does mark a decided change in the public awareness of jazz as an art existing on its own terms. One of the many alleged causes of the collapse of the big-bands was the throng of jazz fanciers (mostly young men) who would stand in front of the band, applauding their idols and crowding out the dancers. The dancers left; the jazz fans stayed.

On June 23rd, at the Civic Auditorium in Pasadena, Gene Norman included Stan Getz in a bill consisting of the King Cole Trio, drummer Louie Bellson and three swing stars – trumpeter Charlie Shavers, altoist Willie Smith and vibraphonist Red Norvo. It is worth noting that this was a racially mixed group (Getz, Norvo and Bellson were white, the others all African-Americans), at a time when such things were by no means common. Southern California was at this time notorious for its degree of unofficial but spitefully enforced segregation.

The Getz who emerges on these recordings is a poised and mature artist. Predictably enough, the complete performances are pretty rambling affairs, but two of his solos stand out as models of cohesion and balance. He has only eight bars on a version of 'Body And Soul', but makes a clear, concise statement in that limited space, a delicate alternative melody of which Lester Young would have approved. Anyone hearing this for the first time, together with the following 'How High The Moon', would be forced to admit that here was something quite new. Perhaps because the prevailing style of the session is straight swing, the Pres element is stronger than usual here, but this is nothing like the careful pastiche displayed with Kai's Krazy Kats, 18 months earlier. Getz's two choruses on the mid-tempo 'How High The Moon' have the graceful fluency of a style at ease with itself and, even though some of the vocabulary is still Lester Young's, there is no doubt that we are hearing a truly distinctive voice. Things take a turn for the worse in the final number, 'Charlie's Got Rhythm', where the tempo, a gale-force 72 bars a minute, catches Getz off-balance. He hangs on by stringing together a series of standard phrases, or 'licks', and manages to scramble through four choruses without undue mishap, but only just. It would be some years before he felt entirely happy with very fast tempos.

The following month, Getz and several of his freelance circle, including Herbie Steward and Shorty Rogers, joined a seven-piece band under the leadership of baritone saxophonist Butch Stone. It was an excellent band but never busy enough, or well-paid enough, to hold onto its musicians. Always on the lookout for work, Getz and Steward finally came across the answer to the under-employed musician's prayer – a bandleader with a gig but no band. This was Tommy DeCarlo, a trumpet player, and he had just signed a contract to provide the band at Pete Pontrelli's Spanish Ballroom in East Los Angeles. Not only was he in urgent need of a band, he also required arrangements for them to play. For these he turned to the trumpeter, pianist and arranger Gene Roland, who had been experimenting with the blend of four cool tenor saxophones for some time, first in New York and later in Los Angeles. In fact, Getz had played in his daytime rehearsal groups in both cities. The regular tenor players at Roland's Los Angeles sessions were Getz, Steward, Zoot Sims and Jimmy Giuffre. DeCarlo recruited all four, thus acquiring a ready-made saxophone section with a unique sound.

By 1947 the normal configuration of a saxophone section had settled down into the form it retains to this day – two altos, two tenors and one baritone. When playing in close harmony, they are usually deployed (reading downwards on the musical score): alto, tenor, alto, tenor, baritone. This produces the bright, surging sound commonly thought of as 'big-band saxes'. There are other ways of setting them out (Ellington, for instance, often placed the baritone above the second tenor), but that is the norm. The closest way to harmonise the instruments is in four parts, all moving in parallel, with the baritone doubling the lead and octave below to make the fifth part. This was the idea that Gene Roland adapted for his all-tenor sections. But why write for four tenors in the first place? The answer lies once more in that delayed-action Lester Young effect. Not only had Pres captivated the Getz generation, he had imbued the tenor saxophone itself with glamour. A lot of young guys were taking up the tenor, emulating Pres, working on the sound and on being cool. As Jimmy Giuffre, an old friend of Gene Roland, told it: "[Gene] went to New York and used to hang out at Nola Studios, where all the young musicians went, and he told me about these hundreds of Lester-type tenor players that were coming along. Every day they were up there at Nola, rehearsing and trying out new things, and he was writing arrangements for them."[4]

The ranges of the various saxophones overlap quite considerably, but a note played on an alto will have a very different tonal quality from the same note on a tenor. Or, to put it another way, a tenor playing at the top of its range does not sound at all like an alto playing in its comfortable middle register. As Gene Roland discovered, the sound of four light-toned tenors in close harmony has a kind of edgy beauty that no other combination can touch, partly because the one playing the lead part is up there in alto territory. In the DeCarlo band Stan Getz played lead.

Pontrelli's was by no means the obvious place to launch a band with an original sound. As Zoot Sims remembered: "That was a funny gig. It was a Mexican ballroom. East Side LA. It was Mexicans, and we played Mexican stocks [standard printed arrangements]. We'd play their music, which we didn't mind doing … but then we'd slip in our own music, and they didn't mind it, so it worked out fine."[5] Gene Roland played piano in the band and Beverly Getz was the vocalist.

THE NEW HERD

Meanwhile, Woody Herman was finding life away from the bandstand increasingly tedious. Although he had broken up his band in December 1946, at the time of the great collapse, it had been for personal rather than financial reasons. Herman's wife, Charlotte, had become an alcoholic and he needed to be at home to support her through her recovery. The Woody Herman orchestra was one of the few reasonably healthy bands at the time he broke it up, with good bookings well into the following year. It was also one of the most exciting big bands in the entire history of jazz, playing music that was advanced for its time, but with such exuberance of spirit that only the dullest of souls could listen to it and not feel invigorated. At the time of the band's demise, its writers, Neal Hefti and Ralph Burns, had found a way of introducing the bebop vocabulary without dampening its high-spirited style, and star soloists like trombonist Bill Harris, tenor saxophonist Flip Phillips and trumpeter Sonny Berman simply revelled in the challenge.

Metronome magazine echoed the feelings of many in its obituary notice for Herman's First Herd, as it came to be known: "Woody Herman's magnificent band is dead. *Requiescat in Pace*. And forgive me if I brush away a tear... Only once before was a band of such unequivocal standards and evenness of musicianship organised. That was the Ellington band. It still is, but Herman is not."[6]

The band business was going from bad to worse, but Herman simply could not stay away. By the summer of 1947 he was planning a new band, a Second Herd, to take over where the First had left off. His right-hand man in scouting for talent was Ralph Burns, who called in at Pontrelli's one night to hear this four-tenor band his friends had told him about. He recognised its potential at once and urged Woody to get over to East LA and hear for himself. Within a few days Herman had hired all four – Getz, Sims and Steward to play, and Giuffre to write arrangements. He already had Serge Chaloff fixed to play baritone and an altoist, Sam Marowitz, as section leader. Other members included trumpeters Shorty Rogers, Ernie Royal and Bernie Glow, trombonist Earl Swope, and Don Lamond on drums.

"Woody's new band is going to be even greater than his last one was," enthused *Metronome*. "It's going to blow exciting, modern jazz and it's going to have a book of wonderful, progressive arrangements."[7] The new band played its first date in San Bernadino, on October 16th 1947, followed by a fairly extensive tour. It was well received and the prospects looked quite good.

Throughout the latter part of 1947 a pay dispute raged between the AFM and the record industry. The union threatened a strike, the companies called their bluff and an indefinite stoppage was called, to begin on January 1st 1948. Recording studios worked overtime in the remaining weeks to build up a stockpile of material. Herman's band went into Columbia's LA studio four times in December 1947. On the 27th they recorded two three-hour sessions, each of which resulted in a jazz classic. The first, Giuffre's 'Four Brothers', was to turn the cool-tenor sound from a hip saxophonists' cult into a worldwide phenomenon. The second, Burns's 'Summer Sequence IV', began the process that would make Stan Getz into a jazz icon.

'Four Brothers' is a brilliant, three-and-a-half-minute display of Woody Herman's new sound at its most irresistibly glamorous and seductive, a mini-concerto grosso in which the three tenors and baritone conduct a dialogue with the full orchestra. The theme itself is rather like a bebop line, but with less jagged contours, and the tonal blend is so close that they really do sound like brothers. The solos (Sims, Chaloff, Steward, Getz – in that order) flow gracefully from one to another, so that they seem to be picking up each other's thoughts. Outside the work of Duke Ellington, 'Four Brothers' stands as one of the rare undisputed masterpieces of jazz composition.

"Woody asked me to write something featuring the tenors, so I did," said Giuffre. "I gave it to Shorty Rogers to take to rehearsal and Woody liked it, but he wasn't sure it was right for his band. He was worried that 'Four Brothers' was too cool and laid back. But the band enjoyed playing it and the saxophone section worked on it together. It got so they could stand up and play the whole thing from memory, but still Woody wouldn't call it on gigs much. Later, when the record was due for release, Woody told Shorty, 'You know which one Columbia likes best? "Four Brothers"!...' Like he still couldn't quite understand it."[8]

The other notable piece recorded that day, 'Summer Sequence IV', was written by Burns as an additional movement to his original three-part *Summer Sequence* concert suite, composed the previous year. The work as it stood was not long enough to fill a side of one of the new long-playing discs, soon to be launched. The new section runs for just over three minutes, at a moderate 20 bars a minute, and Getz's contribution occupies a mere eight bars, but it is so startlingly unlike any previous recorded tenor saxophone solo that it attracted instant attention. The word 'ethereal' has often been applied to it. It drifts up from the body of orchestral sound, hangs weightlessly for a few moments and dissolves into the air. Anyone who had been following his development closely would have recognised it as Getz's work, but it must be remembered that this was his first featured appearance with a major band on a major record label, and Columbia Records had subsidiaries in many foreign countries. People who listened to it because it was the latest Woody Herman disc, who had never heard of Stan Getz, for whom Lester Young was little more than a name, who knew nothing of bebop and were untouched by the metaphysic of cool, heard it and were mesmerised.

The Second Herd was not a well-behaved band. Apart from the disorderly conduct, unsavoury habits and general rascality to be expected from a pack of young men living and travelling together, there was the matter of heroin addiction. It affected at least half the band. Some, like Stan Getz, were already addicted and others became addicts, largely through the efforts of Serge Chaloff, who acted as supplier. In the beginning, Woody had no idea of the extent of the problem, and could not understand why musicians kept falling asleep at rehearsals. They would then take amphetamines to wake themselves up. "That band," he remarked later, "was on everything but roller-skates."

There was still a powerful glamour attached to membership of a big-name band and Getz, at the age of 20, was a dark, good-looking, sweet-faced young man. "Girls would be lining up to meet Stan," remembered vibraphonist Terry Gibbs. "And when we were at the Hollywood Palladium it was more like a movie parade – not just little hopefuls and starlets but real stars. I'm talking about people like Ava Gardner. He could have his pick. But many times, come the end of the set, Stan's gone. He's ignored them all and gone to meet his [drug] connection..."[9]

Herbie Steward left the band quite early in its life. The reason he gave was the constant travelling, which he said disagreed with him, but the drug-fuelled antics of his colleagues may have had something to do with it. Sometimes these could be very funny, such as the episode of Serge Chaloff and the hotel door. The bad boys had all got hold of air pistols and were in Chaloff's room, using the door for target practice. The following day, as they they were about to check out, the manager demanded that Chaloff pay $24 to replace the door, which, after much protestation and bluster, he did. Chaloff then said, "I've paid for the door, so now it's mine. I want it." He stood over the staff while they took the defaced door off its hinges, then he and Terry Gibbs carried it out to the band bus.

Herbie Steward's replacement was Al Cohn, another young, cool tenor player, who was also an up-and-coming arranger. He too soon became addicted. "Everybody in the band was crazy for Al Cohn. When Al played it was always something special... Stan would look up at Al with those blue eyes of his and just stare at him when he was playing. This is Stan Getz, and he's pretty snappy himself."[10]

Pretty snappy and pretty obnoxious, too. Herman's young players all assumed a lofty disdain for the musical efforts of their elders, but Stan Getz carried youthful arrogance to extremes. They all thought Herman's clarinet playing corny and old-fashioned, but it was Getz who actually told Woody, "You play the worst!" To which Woody replied, "Of course I do, you schmuck. That's why I'm paying you – so keep your mouth shut!"

Getz was always indulged, because of his gift, but he was not generally liked. Ralph Burns summed it up bluntly. "Stan was a prick," he said, "but he could play."[11]

SERIOUS MUSIC

The AFM recording ban wore on throughout 1948, making Herman's task even harder. The only studio recordings of the Second Herd come from the very beginning of its life and near to the end. For the rest we have to rely on transcriptions of live broadcasts from ballrooms and nightclubs. These reveal that even a band like Herman's was obliged to pad its programme out with novelty numbers, comedy vocals and suchlike stuff. Night after night they would grind out a kitsch big-band version of Khachaturian's 'Sabre Dance' and Woody would go into his cod-Mexican number, 'My Pal Gonzales'. But despite this, and despite the ever-present distraction of making drug connections, the serious music always came first.

"Sometimes Woody would get off the bandstand for the last set and go home," remembered pianist Lou Levy. "We'd drag out all the arrangements we really loved to play, like Johnny Mandel's 'Not Really The Blues', and play them. There was so much we loved to play in that band. We'd find a piano in some room down in the bowels of a theatre and jam between shows – Al, Zoot, Stan, everybody. We may have had some unhealthy habits, but the music sounded healthy. Whatever else suffered, the music never did."[12]

The band continued touring throughout 1948, and in October, while it was in New York playing a month-long engagement at the Royal Roost, Getz recorded a session as leader of a quintet. The recording strike was still in force, although an end was in sight, and this was a clandestine affair for a tiny label, Sittin' In With, owned by jazz entrepreneur Bob Shad. The idea was to have product ready for release as soon as the dispute was over. The band included Al Haig, a member of Charlie Parker's quintet with the reputation of being the best contemporary rhythm-section pianist. On guitar was Jimmy Raney, currently with Herman. Bass and drums were Clyde Lombardi and Charlie Perry. This is the first appearance of the Getz-Raney partnership which was to blossom in the early 1950s, and the style is uncompromising bebop, as three of the titles suggest: 'As I Live And Bop', 'Pardon My Bop', 'Interlude In Bebop'.

Getz reverts somewhat to the style of the Just Jazz recording, or even of the Vido Musso date, playing a fluid, sinuous line filled with bebop phraseology and delivered completely deadpan, without expressive inflections of any kind. 'As I Live And Bop', a tricky 32-bar theme based on the changes of Charlie Parker's 'Confirmation', provides a fascinating early glimpse of the Getz-Raney partnership and the suave blend of tenor saxophone and electric guitar which they were to perfect. Getz's best performance comes in the first take of the final number of the session, sometimes entitled 'Diaper Pin' and sometimes 'Pin Head'. Little importance was attached to titles at sessions like this, with two takes of the same tune often coming out under different titles. 'Diaper Pin'/'Pin Head' does not actually have a theme; it consists of Getz improvising one-and-a-half choruses on the changes of 'That Old Black Magic'. The skill with which he hints at the original melody by touching it lightly with a few notes from time to time, the relaxed assurance of his manner, the mobility and sheer inventiveness of his line, all these add up to an inspired piece of work.

The strike was finally settled and Herman signed with Capitol Records. In December 1948, almost exactly a year after the 'Four Brothers' session, the band spent two days in the Capitol studios and recorded seven numbers. Two of these, 'Lemon Drop' and 'Early Autumn', would make a particular impression. Immediately the recording ban was lifted, bebop enjoyed a brief popular craze. Like all crazes, it settled on a few easily identifiable characteristics and worked them remorselessly, establishing Dizzy Gillespie as the trend leader. The phenomenon is well characterised by musicologist and historian Scott DeVeaux: "Like swing before it, Gillespie's bebop represented the successful mass marketing of musical (and cultural) practices that had previously circulated in a much narrower ambit. Even when transformed into mainstream entertainment, bebop was still a music with a strong subcultural resonance ... The insider atmosphere was part of the new music's commercial appeal."[13]

Scat singing, weird chords, occasional sartorial trappings like beret and dark glasses, these were the easily identifiable elements of pop-bebop. But, to be fair, pop-bebop did produce some charming, high-spirited records, and 'Lemon Drop' is one of them – a frantic, crazy affair of screaming brass, fleeting solos and manic, wordless vocals. It ends with two voices, Shorty Rogers and Terry Gibbs, one very high and one very low, intoning the theme, and it was this gimmick that caught the public ear and made the record a minor hit.

The other significant Herman recording from December 1948 is 'Early Autumn', a reworking of 'Summer Sequence IV' with Getz more prominently featured and sounding, if anything, even more airy and insubstantial. He takes the last solo, including the coda, so his tenor is the last sound we hear, casting an autumnal glow over everything that has gone before.

In January 1949, the name of Stan Getz appeared for the first time in the *Metronome* readers' poll, in tenth place. He had also become a father for the first time, an event which often turns the thoughts of touring musicians towards the idea of coming in off the road. It would only be a matter of time before Stan Getz gave up being a sideman in anyone's band, even Woody Herman's, and branched out as a leader in his own right. His mind was made up in February, when a bizarre accident proved to be the last straw.

Getz, Chaloff and Burns were driving to a Herman engagement when their car broke down. The band's manager arranged for an express train to be flagged down for them at a wayside station. They clambered aboard, to be greeted with hostile stares and muttering from the other passengers. It turned out that the train's brakeman had jumped down onto the track as the train was coming to a halt, slipped on a patch of ice and fallen under the wheels. He was killed instantly, and had been only a few weeks away from retirement. "Of course, it was an accident, and nobody can blame anybody for it," Getz said later, "but I just got disgusted and quit."[14] After working out his notice, he left at the end of March.

CHAPTER 5

Long Island
Sound

"I can play different styles ... It's fun swingin' and getting 'hot' for a change instead of trying to be cool ... I can be a real stompin' tenor man."

STAN GETZ, AROUND 1950

The Second Herd struggled on through 1949, but it was losing so much money that Herman was forced to call a halt in November, by which time most of the original team had departed. Terry Gibbs and Zoot Sims left in February, Getz and Al Cohn in March, and the spirit slowly ebbed away. Nevertheless, the veterans, now settled in New York, tended to stick together. A popular feature of many big-bands was the small jazz group, or 'band within a band', which would play a few numbers during the course of an evening.

The small band in Herman's orchestras was always called the Woodchoppers, and in the Second Herd this had consisted of Getz, Gibbs, Shorty Rogers and Earl Swope, plus the rhythm section. So when Terry Gibbs landed a session as leader for the recently launched New Jazz label he promptly sent for Getz, Swope and Rogers to join him, along with pianist George Wallington, bassist Curly Russell and drummer Shadow Wilson. Since this is Gibbs's session, he takes the most prominent part in Rogers's hastily sketched arrangements, and often the longest solo too. There is no doubting his virtuosity or the

The manically energetic Horace Silver, who teamed up with Getz in 1950

resourcefulness of his invention, but it is Getz who catches the ear every time. Even at barely 22 years of age he seems to have an inborn authority. The critic Ira Gitler recalled a conversation about this session with the producer and proprietor of New Jazz, Bob Weinstock, and gained "a clear impression that Getz being dissatisfied with his solo on a particular number carried far more weight toward cutting another take than if it had been another member of the cast."[1] Certainly his solos on all three versions of 'Michelle' (a thumbnail score on the changes of 'You Go To My Head') are almost nonchalant in their graceful simplicity. The only time his imperturbable cool becomes ruffled is in 'Cuddles' and 'Speedway', two verisons of the same theme, based on the changes of 'I Got Rhythm', which clock in at around 84 bars a minute, an insane tempo guaranteed to defeat anyone except Charlie Parker.

Thanks to 'Four Brothers' and other Herman records, the silky tenors-in-close-harmony sound had become widely known and admired among modern jazz fans, and strongly associated with the names of Getz, Sims and Cohn. Figuring, no doubt, that five would be even better than three, Weinstock added two further tenors, Allen Eager and Brew Moore, for a session in April. The effect is probably very close to the kind of thing Gene Roland had worked on at Nola Studios back in 1946, with squads of eager young Lester Young disciples. Four numbers were recorded, two ('Battleground' and 'Battle Of The Saxes') written by Al Cohn and two ('Five Brothers' and 'Four And One Moore') by Gerry Mulligan. Squeezing five parts into the tenor saxophone range proved a tight fit and Getz plays baritone during the ensemble passages of 'Five Brothers'.

It is fascinating to hear how alike they all sound, especially in light of their later lives. Here they are stylish young men, playing music at the leading edge of fashion and consciously part of a 'movement'. As they matured, each one developed an individual and unmistakable voice. The Getz of, say, 1970 was utterly different from the Sims of 1970, and neither could be mistaken for Cohn or Moore. Eager, who had a private fortune, gave up music in the mid-1950s, making occasional, half-hearted return forays in later years.

A further session in May, for the Savoy label, finds Getz, Sims and Cohn, along with ex-Hermanites Earl Swope and Jimmy Raney, performing four Al Cohn compositions. It's altogether a more focused affair, with the tenors sounding immaculately Brotherly and Swope's trombone acting as a kind of surrogate baritone. The recording quality is better too. Getz is the featured soloist, although each one has his moment, and Cohn's writing is already showing signs of the successful composer-arranger he was later to become. On this occasion all four numbers – 'Stan Getz Along', 'Stan's Mood', 'Slow' and 'Fast' – demonstrate his gift for creating clear, ringing and deceptively simple melodies, a talent which is also evident in his improvisation. 'Stan's Mood', a showpiece for Getz, is particularly effective. With severely limited resources Cohn devises a warmly textured backdrop in the style of 'Early Autumn', to which Getz responds with a wonderfully limpid solo line.

Getz continued recording with ad hoc bands, under various leaders but drawn largely from the Haig-Raney-Winding circle, through 1949. Despite his rising reputation among aficionados, he found the going tough to begin with. Even in New York City the number of clubs offering modern jazz was limited, and virtually every big name was available for them to choose from. On one occasion he was reduced to taking a job with a marching band in the Communist Party's May Day parade, for a fee of ten dollars. This was the period of the anti-communist witch-hunts and the parade automatically became the focus of abuse. "There was a loyalty parade on Sixth Avenue, by the American Legion," recalled Getz, "and the Commies had theirs on Eighth Avenue. For ten dollars you marched all the way down Broadway, and you turned at 34th Street onto Eighth Avenue and on down to Washington Square, where you'd collect your ten dollars. All the way down people were throwing pieces of wood at us and spitting at us. And as we turned right on 34th Street, playing the 'Internationale', this one trumpet player kept walking straight on, out of the band and right out of the parade, and he was shouting, 'To hell with the ten dollars!'."[2]

And then, in July, Herman's 'Early Autumn' was released and things began to change. Getz could have made any number of records for New Jazz or Savoy, been the idol of every cool cat in the universe, and still be just another saxophone player scratching around for a living. But Capitol was a major label, with major distribution, and the effect was similar to that of 'Summer Sequence IV', only more so. This time, the names of Terry Gibbs and Stan Getz appeared on the record label itself, which meant that disc-jockeys mentioned them. From tenth place in the *Metronome* poll at the start of 1949, Getz shot to Number One tenor in January 1950 and was named 'Musician Of The Year', while in the Down Beat poll he jumped from tenth to second. "Not since the big years of Coleman Hawkins, and the succeeding success of Lester Young," said the *Metronome Year-Book*, "has a tenor man hit musicians so hard and reached so firmly into the hearts and heads of jazz fans."[3]

Shortly before the release of 'Early Autumn', Getz was signed up to record as leader of a quartet by Prestige, the parent company of Bob Weinstock's New Jazz. The tenor-and-rhythm quartet became a standard jazz instrumentation only in the mid-1940s, when Lester Young used it for some of his finest work. It was Lester's quartet records for Keynote and Savoy that had captivated Getz as a teenage musician, and always remained his preferred medium. He regarded it, he once said, as "the jazz equivalent of the string quartet".[4] Not only did he adopt Lester Young's instrumentation, he also drew from the same body of material, the rich treasury of classic American song.

NEW VOICE

Since most of Getz's recorded work comes from that source, the classic American song, this would be a good moment to introduce a few remarks on the subject. From the mid-1920s until at least the late 1960s, the overwhelming bulk of jazz performance was based on two forms – the 12-bar blues and the 32-bar American song. This applies to original themes as well as to pieces with the word 'blues' in the title, or those bearing the title of a popular song. Gershwin's 'I Got Rhythm' (shorn of its two-bar coda) serves as the basis of literally countless jazz pieces from the swing and bebop eras. Most of Charlie Parker's tricky and complex themes are based on the harmonies, or 'changes', of songs like 'Indiana' (Parker's 'Donna Lee'), 'Cherokee' ('Ko-Ko'), 'Embraceable You' ('Quasimodo'), and so on. We have already encountered Stan Getz recordings such as 'Pin Head' ('That Old Black Magic'), 'Opus De Bop' ('I Got Rhythm') and 'Five Brothers' ('Rose Of The Rio Grande').

Stan Getz NOBODY ELSE BUT ME

This building of themes on the foundations of popular songs, or even launching straight into the improvisation without stating a theme of any kind, was a characteristic bebop practice. It required great ingenuity and, almost as important, it allowed the musician to claim the composer credit, at the same time saving the record company from having to pay royalties to Cole Porter, Irving Berlin or the estate of George Gershwin. Thus, artistic endeavour and financial prudence found themselves in happy accord. But the vast majority of jazz performances, live or recorded, continued to be straightforward expositions and elaborations of popular songs, the most commonly used being known as 'standards'. This is still normal practice over much of the jazz world today.

It is impossible to imagine the history of jazz without the American song, just as it is impossible to imagine the American song without jazz. They are not separate entities, but parts of the same thing: the musical and verbal expression of a huge and disparate nation in a period of dynamic growth and served by mass communications. It should not be necessary to labour such an obvious point, but histories of jazz have often been strangely coy on this subject. The reason could well lie somewhere in the effort to establish jazz as a 'serious' art, or as a 'music of protest' – in either case not to be associated with bourgeois stuff from Hollywood musicals and Broadway shows. It could equally well be part of some doomed attempt to write white people out of jazz history altogether. In recent times jazz has become an adventure playground for crackpots and fanatics of all kinds, but the prime importance of the American song in jazz is verifiable by the simple act of picking up a miscellaneous handful of jazz CDs and reading the list of contents.

'Early Autumn' established Stan Getz as a major new voice in jazz, and the subsequent stream of quartet records consolidated his position. For the first Prestige session, on June 21st 1949, he was accompanied by Al Haig, with Gene Ramey on bass and Stan Levey on drums. Six titles were recorded, although one was discarded and seems to have vanished without trace. The five released titles make an interesting selection: one American ballad, Victor Herbert's 'Indian Summer', which had been a hit record for Tommy Dorsey and Frank Sinatra ten years earlier; Getz's own 'Long Island Sound', a very close paraphrase of the old Judy Garland number 'Zing! Went The Strings Of My Heart'; Getz's 'Mar-cia', a considerably less close paraphrase of EA Swan's 'When Your Lover Has Gone'; and a pair of blues improvisations, 'Prezervation' and 'Crazy Chords'. These two were clearly put there to frighten lesser musicians. Each one is 13 choruses long and each chorus is in a different key, starting and fininshing in E-flat. 'Prezervation' moves from one key to another by resolving upwards in fourths (E-flat, A-flat, D-flat, G-flat etc), while 'Crazy Chords' moves upwards by semitones (E-flat, E, F, F-sharp etc). For non-musicians, it should be pointed out here that it is customary for jazz pieces to be pitched in a range of about seven common keys, and so to ask someone to play the blues in F-sharp would not normally be construed as a friendly act. To enliven matters even further, both numbers are taken at around 72 bars a minute. Neither Getz nor Haig falters as they sprint purposefully through this minefield, sounding just as sure-footed in E or B as they do in F or B-flat.

The first of the 78rpm records to be issued (Prestige 710) was 'Long Island Sound' and it did particularly well, especially in the New York area, where the leading jazz disc jockey, Symphony Sid Torin, played it constantly, occasionally turning it over and playing the other side, 'Mar-cia', too. The special appeal of 'Long Island Sound' probably derives from the combination of its angelic, high-pitched sound with the laconic, hide-and-seek approach to the song on which it's based. In this it was exactly right for its time. In the same year, for example, the George Shearing Quintet began a quite phenomenal run of successes with a version of 'September In The Rain', in which virtuosity and a cool, subdued sound are similarly combined.

COOL AND DELICATE

On Christmas Eve 1949, Getz appeared at Carnegie Hall on a bill which reads like one of those dream lists that teenage sports fans tend to make – all the greats in the same team. In this case the list included Charlie Parker, Miles Davis, Sarah Vaughan and Bud Powell, among others. Getz's inclusion confirmed his arrival among the leading figures in the new jazz. Inevitably, he played 'Long Island Sound' and, as is often the case when a musician has been playing a piece over and over for some time, the live recording reveals that he played it at almost double the original tempo.

The second Prestige session, with Haig still on piano and Tommy Potter and Roy Haynes on bass and drums respectively, took place on January 6th 1950. Seven numbers were completed, two of them accompaniments to a vocalist, Junior Parker, which need not detain us. Of the remaining five, four were standards and one a Getz original. The quartet performances have now settled into a simple and effective pattern. Getz plays one chorus of lightly decorated melody and a second chorus of improvisation. This is followed by an improvised chorus from the piano, after which Getz returns for a final chorus, which starts out as improvisation and closes as a partial restatement of the melody. At a moderate tempo of around 48 bars a minute, this fits neatly into the three-minute span of a ten-inch, 78rpm record side. There are variations, of course. The whole thing often starts with a four or eight-bar piano introduction, of which Al Haig was a consummate master. He was able to set tempo and a mood, and even drop a fleeting reference to the coming melody, all in a few seconds. There is a lovely example at the start of 'What's New' from this session.

Of the remaining numbers, 'There's A Small Hotel', 'Too Marvellous For Words' and 'I've Got You Under My Skin', conform exactly to the above pattern. The Getz original, 'Intoit', is unusual in that it begins with a series of introductory flourishes against static chords before settling into the main theme. For the first few bars the unwary listener might be led into expecting a thinly disguised version of 'I Didn't Know What Time It Was', but this is a false trail. The piece is actually based on the changes of Dizzy Gillespie's 'A Night In Tunisia'. It's possible that Getz had in mind a similar joke played by Lester Young in Basie's 1939 recording of 'Taxi War Dance' (loosely based on 'Willow Weep For Me'), where he opens the number with a misleading quote from 'Ol' Man River'.

Being a *Metronome* poll-winner meant being part of the annual *Metronome* All-Stars recording, which took place a few days after the quartet session above. Because each winner had to be featured somewhere on the two 78rpm sides, no-one has much chance to shine, but there are a few moments of characteristic Getz on both 'Double Date' and 'No Figs'. Among the others taking part were Dizzy Gillespie, Kai Winding and Serge Chaloff.

As the stream of quartet recordings continued through 1950, Getz's tone grew ever more delicate, even fragile, and his way with a melody increasingly gentle. If a song is to a jazz musician what a subject is to a painter, then Stan Getz's work in the early 1950s resembles nothing so much as a series of pale and exquisite watercolours. Take, for example, 'My Old Flame', from the Prestige session of April 14th 1950. There are two takes of this and on neither does he stray below the middle of the instrument's range. The entire two choruses (there is no piano interlude this time) are centred in the piping high register. The same is largely true of the other three pieces. Only in the relatively energetic 'The Lady In Red' does he descend occasionally into traditionally tenor territory.

But light of touch though they may be, these quartet numbers display a technical command of astounding completeness. Each little decorative flourish around the melody is brought off with absolute precision. Every turn of the improvised line, every accent, is faultlessly placed and executed. Even such a basic element as intonation, playing in tune, is so accurate that it becomes noticeable. Simply from a technical standpoint, Stan Getz at the age of 23 was already the cause of admiration bordering on despair among other tenor saxophonists.

And yet, as he later admitted, he was scarcely ever sober when playing, and never while recording, and was at the same time supporting a serious heroin habit. None of this was discernable in his manner or in his circumstances. To the casual eye he seemed the very ideal of the rising young professional musician. He was tall, dark and good-looking. He may have seemed a little pale, the result of long nights in jazz clubs, but otherwise was the picture of health. He lived with his wife and small son in his own house in the respectable Long Island suburb of Levittown, from which he commuted to Manhattan and occasionally to other east-coast centres such as Boston. Both Stan and his wife Beverly were addicts, but with their income rising dramatically and everything else going well the problem remained under control. However, early in 1950, Beverly's older brother, Buddy Stewart, died in a car crash, and the shock upset the delicate equilibrium of their lives. From this point the marriage began gradually to fall apart, as Beverly's increasing drug dependency began to make increasing inroads into their everyday lives.

The April 14th session was Getz's last for Bob Weinstock, and he followed it with his first for the Roost label a month later. He did not yet have a regular band of his own but preferred to record with the Haig-Potter-Haynes team. This was not always possible, however, because the three were working regularly as Charlie Parker's rhythm section, travelling with him as part of the 'Charlie Parker with Strings' package. That's why the rhythm section on the 'Lady In Red' session consists of Tony Aless, Percy Heath and Don Lamond. But the full A-Team was available, for the last time as it turned out, on May17th , for the first Roost session.

As is often the case with jazz artists of Getz's stature, there's nothing to choose between an 'accepted' and a 'rejected' take – for example, in this case, takes one and two of 'On The Alamo', both of which have survived. The impression is that he could have continued for hours, happily extemporising on this elegant and robust old song, had it not been for the limitation imposed by the 78rpm format, which was soon to be swept away. The long-playing record was becoming well established in the US by 1950, although mainly for classical music. Recorded jazz still came for the most part in three-minute, jukebox-friendly bites. It was a format which, whatever its drawbacks, concentrated the mind wonderfully. In point of fact, all six pieces from this session come in comfortably under three minutes, except for the positively angelic 'You Go To My Head', which just touches the magic figure.

This date is also noteworthy for including one of the first recorded compositions of Johnny Mandel, then aged 25 and later to become a Grammy Award-winning film composer. The piece, entitled 'Hershey Bar' and often wrongly credited to Getz himself, is noticeably a more carefully crafted tune than the average jazz 'original'.

HOT AND SWINGIN'

Predictably, Getz was voted top of the polls again and recorded with the Metronome All-Stars in January 1951. It's interesting to see that almost everyone taking part was a member of what might loosely be termed the 'cool school' – including Miles Davis (whose contemporary nine-piece band was later to be dubbed Birth Of The Cool), George Shearing, alto saxophonist Lee Konitz, and four ex-Hermanites: Getz, Winding, Chaloff and Gibbs.

Not having his own band meant that when Getz travelled out of New York to appear at a jazz club he would be accompanied by the resident or 'house' rhythm section. This practice was, and still is, generally accepted, and bears a certain resemblance to Russian roulette. Unless he knows the musicians personally or by reputation, the soloist has no way of telling whether he is in for a swinging, creative evening or a few hours of musical ditch-digging. When Getz travelled to Hertford, Connecticut, in the summer of 1950 he found himself teamed with a truly inspiring trio, led by a young pianist named Horace Silver. At the end of the engagement Getz told them he would send for them to join him in New York. "We'd heard the same thing from other guys who came to play at the club," Silver recalled. "Lucky Thompson said he'd call us, but he never did." [5] But Getz was as good as his word and, on December 10th 1950, all three – Silver, bassist Joe Calloway and drummer Walter Bolden – joined him in the studio to record seven numbers for Roost.

Anyone familiar with Silver's later work, in particular the glorious sequence of Blue Note albums by his own quintet, recorded from the late 1950s through the 1960s, will recognise his touch on the piano and the quirky humour in his style. Ebullient and outgoing, possessed of a seemingly endless supply of manic energy, Horace Silver was the opposite of cool and, even at this formative stage, clearly his own man. A player less like the unruffled Al Haig it would be difficult to imagine, but Getz instantly took to the young Silver and recognised his vast potential.

The recordings with Silver mark a definite warming of the climate. From that first session comes an absolutely blistering 'Strike Up The Band', in which Getz plays with an assertiveness and all-round brio that is a world away from the languid crooning of the 'Lady In Red' session of eight months before. He even interpolates a Silver-style bugle call into his solo. The new pianist's cheeriness was obviously catching. But the most impressive aspect of a piece like 'Strike Up The Band' is the sheer burnished perfection of Getz's performance. The phrases spin out effortlessly, but they also balance and echo one another. Each note, no matter how fleeting, is enunciated with sharp precision. This is jazz saxophone playing of such a high order that considerations of style or period are beside the point. John Coltrane once said, after listening to Getz, "We'd all sound like that if we could," and that has been the general opinion among saxophonists for decades.

As to coolness, there is the evidence of his own words that Getz was finding the 'cool' label irksome and beginning to worry about the danger of being type-cast. "I can play different styles," he protested to an interviewer at around this time. "It's fun swingin' and getting 'hot' for a change instead of trying to be cool. I don't want to become stagnant. I can be a real stompin' tenor man..." [6]

The second session with Silver, Calloway and Bolden took place the following month and included two of Silver's own compositions, 'Penny' and 'Split Kick'. Since he was soon to become the celebrated composer of such jazz standards as 'The Preacher', 'Doodlin', 'Opus De Funk' and 'Sister Sadie', this is an important landmark in his career. It is also an early example of Getz's readiness to take the compositions of young bandmembers into his repertoire. Few star soloists or bandleaders have been as adventurous, or as generous, as Stan Getz in this regard. He seems to have been governed by what we might call, to use a high-flown term, his artistic conscience. He had many problems and distractions – his own addiction, his wife's addiction, his permanently indigent parents, not to mention all the pressures of sudden success. The easy thing would have been to hire a band of reliable journeymen and tour the country, playing selections from his recent records and concluding each show with 'Early Autumn' and 'Long Island Sound'. But it would have been a living death and he could never have brought himself to do it.

STANDINAVIA

Early in 1951, the promoter Norman Granz approached Getz with an offer to join his Jazz At The Philharmonic touring package on its first European trip. Getz agreed and some preliminary publicity was released, but the arrangement collapsed and the plan was aborted. However, the organiser who had been due to book the show in Sweden judged that a visit by Stan Getz would be a viable proposition and invited him to play a week of dates in Stockholm and Gothenburg. He arrived on March 18th, to be greeted at the airport by a cheering crowd and the promoter bearing a bouquet of flowers. Like all American jazz musicians visiting Europe for the first time in the 1950s/early 1960s, he was at first taken aback and then overwhelmed by the warmth of the reception. From being a minority interest confined to record enthusiasts and a few members of the intelligentsia before the war, jazz in Europe had grown into something like an obsession among young people from many classes of society. Apart from the obvious appeal of the music itself, there was the fact that jazz had been condemned by the Nazis, along with modern painting, sculpture and literature, as *entartete Kunst* (degenerate art) and therefore identified with liberation and the free spirit. This was true even in neutral Sweden.

Prestige and Roost recordings were readily available through licensing deals with European labels such as Metronome (Sweden), Blue Star (France) and Esquire (Great Britain). They had been reviewed and discussed in a lively musical press, with such enthusiasm and attention to detail that Getz would soon have found himself in the same position as other American musicians who confessed that their European fans knew more about their recorded careers than they knew themselves.

Getz was by no means the first. Charlie Parker had visited Sweden a few months earlier and caused a sensation, but the sheer vastness of his talent and the exotic otherness of the man himself had engulfed and even terrified many of his listeners. "We were well-brought-up lads," admitted saxophonist Ingmar Glanzelius sadly, "and lacked Parker's fury." [7] The Getz of 'Long Island Sound', on the other hand – with that they could feel some kinship.

Getz recorded two sessions for *Metronome* in Stockholm with Swedish musicians, notably the pianist Bengt Hallberg, whose light, crystalline touch is reminiscent of Al Haig, but softer. The numbers include a charming version of an old Swedish song, 'Ack Varmeland Du Skona', later recorded by Miles Davis and others under the title 'Dear Old Stockholm'. Three of the pieces bear grisly evidence of Getz's fondness for punning titles, in one case two titles for different releases of the same tune, thus adding to the general confusion – namely 'S'Cool Boy' (aka 'Stan Gets Bengt') from the first session. From the second, which also features Sweden's baritone saxophone star Lars Gullin, comes the blues entitled 'Don't Getz Scared'. This apparently proved too much for some sensibilities, and certain releases give it as 'Don't Get Scared', or even 'Don't Be Afraid'. Finally, for its first US and British releases, 'Varmeland' was renamed 'Standinavian'.

The brief Swedish visit did wonders for Getz's reputation in Europe, elevating him from the status of a theoretical or disembodied hero, known only from records, into the solid, genuine article. Cool jazz was still a minority cult, but the minority was a sizeable and noticeable one and Stan Getz was its adopted figurehead. Indeed, all over Europe young jazz lovers were taking up instruments in unprecedented numbers, seeking to emulate their heroes. It was reported that the great Norwegian soprano Kirsten Flagstad had been spotted in Manny's, the New York instrument store, asking for a tenor saxophone mouthpiece (just like Stan Getz's), at the urgent request of her nephew.

Returning to New York, Getz decided to include the ex-Herman guitarist Jimmy Raney in his future plans. The two had always got on well, both personally and musically, and had worked together, on and off, since leaving Herman. The tenor saxophone and the electric guitar, the two characteristic instruments of the 20th century, have an uncanny affinity. Played as a 'single line' instrument (one note at a time) the guitar's sound closely matches that of the tenor, while as a chordal accompaniment it envelops the saxophone without overwhelming it. Raney was a master single-line player, whose melodic ideas ran along very similar lines to Getz's. His full-chord playing, heard less often, is subtle and delicate. Together, as leading figures of the Stan Getz Quintet, they were to make some of the finest music of Getz's career.

Their first recording as the Quintet dates from August 1951, and it is clear from the outset that this is to be a more structured affair than the Quartet had ever been. Horace Silver is still at the piano, but Calloway and Bolden have gone, to be replaced by Leonard Gaskin on bass and Getz's favourite drummer at the time, Roy Haynes. Three of the numbers are new pieces by Gigi Gryce, a young saxophonist who had studied composition in Paris with both Nadia Boulanger and Arthur Honegger. At 23, Gryce was a few months younger than Getz and this represented his first major exposure as a jazz writer. The themes, 'Melody Express', 'Wildwood' and 'Yvette' are all attractive tunes, backed by mobile but not unnecessarily complex changes. They suit the timbre of unison tenor and guitar so well that they were almost certainly created with that specific sound in mind. Perhaps the most memorable of the three is 'Wildwood', which begins with a faint echo of 'Singin' In The Rain', but later makes a few snazzy passes with off-centre phrasing. Getz negotiates the transition from theme statement to solo with an off-hand elegance that is exceptional, even for him.

There is a quite noticeable alteration in his tone here, compared with the Swedish recordings. A harder, more edgy sound has replaced the soft, fluting timbre. The most likely explanation would be a change of mouthpiece, although one cannot be sure. The mouthpiece is crucial in the production of an individual sound and, once they have settled on one that suits them, most saxophonists hang on to it with grim determination. But pictures taken throughout his career show that Getz changed mouthpieces fairly often. The difficulty lies in determining when he was using which mouthpiece, since photographs are often undated, and lining that information up with a specific recording. In any case, mouthpieces come in a range of internal dimensions, invisible from the outside, and two players can produce entirely different sounds from identical mouthpieces. Even so, sudden changes in tone are often the result of mouthpiece change.

The Stan Getz Quintet was now a regular, established band, available for touring. Horace Silver left, to attend to his burgeoning career in New York, and Al Haig came back to play piano. The bass and drums were Teddy Kotick and Tiny Kahn. The quintet was well received by public and critics alike and Roost decided that its next Getz project should be a live album, recorded specifically for the new, long-playing format, without time limitations. The 78rpm record, repository of jazz since its early beginnings, was finally headed for retirement. The venue chosen was Boston's Storyville Club, the date October 28th 1951. The quintet had been working continuously for almost two months and had reached that stage of comfortable looseness and familiarity with the material which only regular playing can achieve. In the event, the evening yielded enough material for two LPs, 13 numbers that have scarcely been out of print since their first release; 'Volume 1' in 1952 and 'Volume 2' the following year. *Stan Getz At Storyville* is a classic of small-band jazz and a landmark in Getz's career.

CHAPTER 6

Move

"The best way to create something is to get into the 'alpha state' ... what we call 'relaxed concentration' ... The more you tighten up, the worse it gets."

STAN GETZ

It's difficult to know where to begin in praise of Getz's Storyville recordings, but a good place to start might be the quality of the ensemble playing. Long hours of playing together can do wonders for any band, but only the best achieve a state close to abandon, in which anything seems possible. The majority of numbers on this live recording are taken at fast, even ultra-fast, tempos, and the great danger in such circumstances is tenseness. It only takes one member of a band to start tightening up for the strain to communicate itself to the others, yet everyone here is supremely relaxed.

Al Haig stumbles occasionally in the fastest pieces, but shrugs it off. Tiny Kahn, one of the most responsive drummers of his generation, creates an exemplary, flowing beat, constantly adjusting the texture of the drums and cymbals to complement the soloist. Kahn, who also played piano and vibraphone and was an outstanding arranger, died in 1953, at the age of 29, before his talents could be fully appreciated. Fortunately the bass is well recorded and it's possible to hear Teddy Kotick's immaculate line and pinpoint timing clearly enough to understand why Charlie Parker named him among his favourite bass players.

Stan Getz and valve trombonist Bob Brookmeyer, 1953

Stan Getz NOBODY ELSE BUT ME

As for the rapport between Getz and Raney, bassist Bill Crow's description of them as a pair of birds "circling each other in mid-air"[1] catches the impression exactly. There is not a great deal of simultaneous improvisation, but some of the theme statements are little gems of musical unanimity, 'Thou Swell' and 'The Song Is You' in particular. These obviously started out as set, unwritten 'head arrangements', but gradually loosened up to the point where they sound entirely spontaneous. The match between their sounds and the obvious similarity in their musical thought processes are a constant source of delight throughout this session. They both play with such aplomb and apparent ease that it's easy to overlook the virtuosity they bring to the task. It is doubtful if any guitarist has ever surpassed Raney's single-line playing here for fluidity at high speed. As for Getz himself, the soft-toned dreamer has definitely been banished for the evening and a more forceful character stands in his place.

There are times, such as his solo in 'Parker 51', when the sheer facility of his playing is almost beyond belief. 'Parker 51' is a Jimmy Raney composition, based on the changes of Ray Noble's 'Cherokee', a great favourite of Charlie Parker (hence the punning title). It's a 64-bar sequence, arranged in the traditional AABA form – A being the main melody and B the contrasting bridge part. The A sections are deceptively simple, moving around conventionally enough in the key of B-flat, but the B section presents a harmonic obstacle course, beginning with a sudden lurch into B major and working its way back to B-flat over the course of 16 bars. The quintet take it at 84 bars a minute, a suicidal tempo for most people, but Getz sails through as though propelled by a comfortable light breeze, even managing to drop the occasional joke and insert a few sly quotations. He was always a master of the fleeting quote, unlike some players who overdo it by labouring the point with endless nudges and winks. The quotes in 'Parker 51' come and go so quickly that they scarcely register – old favourites like 'Canadian Capers' and Dvořák's 'Humoresque' and other bits and pieces so fragmentary that they might just be accidental.

Except, of course, that none of it is truly accidental, just as nothing is pre-planned – it all happens at a level of concentration beneath ordinary thought, and in a part of the imagination which is purely musical and non-verbal. Like most musicians, Getz could discourse cogently on technical matters to do with playing the saxophone and other practical questions, but where it all came from and how he did what he did remained as much a mystery to him as to everyone else. He did, nonetheless, recognise that it involved a singular mental process, in which "the less you concentrate the better". He called it the 'alpha state'. "The best way to create something is to get into the alpha state... what we call 'relaxed concentration'. For example, an accountant doesn't use the alpha, he just concentrates. The more you tighten up physically and mentally in jazz music, and maybe in most music, the worse it gets."[2] Unfortunately, the most reliable route to the alpha state, for Getz, was by way of drugs and drink.

Almost as headlong as 'Parker 51' is the quintet's treatment of 'Move', Denzil Best's theme on the 'I Got Rhythm' changes, featuring an electrifying exchange of four-bar phrases between Getz and Tiny Kahn. These lead into one of Kahn's very few recorded drum solos, which makes it depressingly clear what a great loss his early death was to jazz. 'Move' is played in its usual key of B-flat. Any tune performed with any regularity tends, as a matter of convenience, to come complete with its generally accepted key, although not everyone sticks to this arrangement. Lester Young often liked to pick his own key, and so did Getz. The version of 'Pennies From Heaven' on the Storyville recording is pitched in D major, instead of the normal C, and 'Thou Swell' is in C, rather than E-flat. In both cases, the new key centres the tune beautifully in the tenor saxophone's range, which was presumably the reason for the change.

More than half a century has passed since this music was played, yet it's hard to believe it was so long ago, and that all the participants are dead. The feeling of exuberance and bursting life that comes from it, even after repeated playings, is quite overwhelming, and this is heightened by the fact that it's a live recording, with an audience present. There is a moment, at the close of Kahn's drum solo on 'Move', when somebody lets out a whoop of pure joy, a sound so fitting that it has now become an inseparable part of the music itself.

There is a fascinating addendum to this classic record. The Stan Getz Quintet was sharing the bill at Storyville that week with Billie Holiday and her trio. (Perhaps we should pause for a moment in contemplation of a vanished world where such things were possible, indeed even commonplace.) The opportunity to play Pres to Lady Day, just once, proved too tempting to miss. The night following his quintet recording, Getz crept on stage and joined Billie for three numbers, 'Ain't Nobody's Business', 'You're Driving Me Crazy' and 'Lover Come Back To Me'. There are no tenor solos, just smooth, sweet, slightly off-mike obbligatos, but the recording captures that unique moment. Inevitably, discs were pressed and put on sale. When Norman Granz, Billie's recording director (and soon to be Getz's too), found out, he ordered the master tape and every available copy to be rounded up and destroyed. Fortunately, he failed.

MOOD SWINGS

By the end of 1951 Getz had been continuously on the road with the quintet for four months. He and Beverly now had two children – their second son, David, had been born in September – and this seemed a good time to live a more settled life for a while. Even without the quintet, the name Stan Getz should have been sufficient to keep him comfortably employed as a freelance soloist. Sufficient, that is, to maintain a reasonable suburban life for a man, his wife and two kids – but not sufficient for all that plus two expensive heroin habits. The apparent solution to this dilemma came from guitarist Johnny Smith, a member of the NBC studio orchestra in New York, who told Stan about an opening there for a saxophonist. He took the job. It might seem odd that a world-famous jazz musician should willingly become an anonymous studio player, but jazz musicians have often done this kind of work, usually as freelances but occasionally on staff. Studio playing at the level Getz was taking on is no job for a harmless, unimaginative drudge. It requires great technique and sight-reading skill, quick reactions, the flexibility to fit in with a wide variety of styles and, for saxophone players, the mastery of several instruments. All this appealed to Getz and he started out full of enthusiasm.

"To me it's great," he told *Down Beat* shortly after joining NBC. "On the *Kate Smith Show*, for instance, I had to play baritone, tenor, clarinet and bass clarinet. On the *Jane Pickens Show* I play clarinet only... The other night I did the *Cameo Television Theater Show*. I was the only musician on it. There I was, all by myself, playing bass clarinet. I had to create some themes, mood music to hold the sequences together."

He even declared his intention of taking up the bassoon again, as well as pointing out that he had a deal to work up to six months of the year at Birdland. And "if I take an offer that comes in to play the summer on the French Riviera, I can take leave of absence from NBC."[3]

In March, he recorded four numbers with Johnny Smith for the Roost label, one of which, 'Moonlight In Vermont' – a gentle treatment of a classic ballad – became an unexpected hit, his biggest since 'Early Autumn'. Indeed the piece is something of a throwback to his pale-watercolour period. The opening theme is played in broad, lush chords by Smith, with Getz tiptoeing gently between the phrases before gradually moving to centre stage. It is an utterly charming performance, just the right length for radio play and promotion as a single. Backed by the very similar 'Where Or When' as its B-side, 'Moonlight In Vermont' was promoted as swoony, romantic background music and scored a success with listeners well outside the core jazz audience. It also served to raise Getz's public profile and attract offers it was difficult to refuse. Soon he found himself spending even less time at home than before joining NBC.

"I would work from 12 to 5 on the *Kate Smith Show*, an afternoon television spectacular, and then catch a plane for Rochester or wherever," said Getz. "So I was working five days and seven nights a week, flying back and forth every day. Or if we were working in, say, Atlantic City, where there's no plane, I'd drive four hours there and back. After a while I just got fed up and gave up the studio work."[4]

He was getting bored anyway and would have given it up sooner or later. Getz and Smith followed up their hit by recording another four numbers in November. Two of them, 'Tenderly' and 'Stars Fell On Alabama', did quite well but not spectacularly. Apart from bringing his tenure with NBC to a close, and causing club-owners to insist he played the tune at least once in every show, 'Moonlight In Vermont' had one far-reaching outcome for Getz. It prompted Norman Granz to offer him a recording contract and to include him in the impressive roster of artists featured in his concert promotions.

Granz was by now the most powerful impresario that jazz had ever seen. Driven by a curious mixture of altruism and ruthlessness, an ardent jazz lover in whom good taste fought a not always successful battle with an oddly philistine streak, a passionate campaigner against racial discrimination, a relentless fighter on behalf of jazz musicians' rights to be treated as serious artists, a man who saw the entire world as a potential audience for his records and his touring concert packages, Granz was a phenomenon. He also paid very well indeed.

During his time with NBC, Getz had been working either as a solo artist, accompanied by house rhythm sections, or with ad hoc quartets and quintets as close as possible in make-up to the band on the Storyville recordings. Al Haig was out of the picture, having left the music business and, apparently, given up playing. He returned to it after a year or so, but maintained a deliberately low profile, playing background piano in cocktail bars and suchlike. It was not until the mid-1970s that Haig finally re-emerged from his shell and began recording and touring again. He died in 1982.

Getz's first choice as Haig's replacement, whenever he could get him, was Duke Jordan, formerly a member of Charlie Parker's quintet and a concise, pithy player of great experience. A parade of temporary bassists and drummers passed through until Getz finally settled on Bill Crow and Frank Isola.

Broadcasts and concert recordings from 1952 reveal that however tired, hung-over or strung-out he may have been, Getz's playing sounded as blithe and airy as ever. A typical example comes from Duke Ellington's 25th anniversary concert at Carnegie Hall on November 14th, with this quintet line-up. As well as the inevitable 'Moonlight In Vermont' (a totally different treatment from the hit version) there is an engagingly high-spirited 'Strike Up The Band', into which Getz contrives to insert quotations from 'Yes, Sir, That's My Baby' and 'Santa Claus Is Coming To Town'. It is noticeable, however, that Getz and Raney play only the final eight bars together, which is sad in view of the rapport demonstrated on the Storyville session only a year previously. Relations between them were becoming strained because of Getz's increasingly unpredictable mood swings, caused by his heroin use. At one moment he would be everybody's jovial pal, and at the next suspicious and abusive.

To a non-addict like Raney, the whole drug scene, with its atmosphere of paranoia and grubby criminality, was abhorrent. He put up with it because he adored Getz's playing and the creative intensity he generated, but it was getting more difficult by the day.

SVEN COOLSON

Getz's first recording session under his contract with Norman Granz took place on December 12th 1952. As a producer, Granz adopted a more hands-on approach than either Prestige's Herman Lubinski or Roost's Teddy Reig. As Getz had just scored a hit with a laid-back version of 'Moonlight...', so Granz decreed that Getz's first session for his Clef label would concentrate on gentle ballads and that he, Granz, would choose them. In the event, the session resulted in six ballads and two up-tempo pieces. Although intended for release on LP, each individual piece was timed to fit a 78 or 45rpm single side.

Unlike Prestige or Roost – both small companies with tight budgets – Granz always used the best recording facilities. The improvement in general sound quality is quite spectacular. Probably for the first time, the whole of Getz is captured – every shading of tone, every nuance of tonguing, the occasional sleight-of-hand with unorthodox fingering – every detail of that immaculate technique is clearly audible. Equally impressive is the casual efficiency with which the technique is deployed, never once displayed for its own sake but equal to any demand made upon it. Getz's rhythmic poise is so secure that the trickiest twists and turns come over as sheer exuberance. A good example occurs in the up-tempo 'The Way You Look Tonight', at the transition from the opening theme to Getz's solo, where he casually bounces a repeated five-note phrase across the bar-lines, pursuing it through the break and four bars into the chorus. This playfulness is one of the most endearing aspects of Getz's musical personality. It reveals itself in rhythmic tricks, sudden deviations from the expected path and, of course, in the ubiquitous quotations: there's a beauty in 'The Way You Look Tonight' – a whole 12 bars of 'Can't Help Lovin' That Man' inserted squarely into the theme statement, as if to say, "See? Clever guy, that Jerome Kern – got away with writing the same tune twice..."

Slow and medium-paced ballads always brought out the melodist in Getz. The pursuit of melody as a prime virtue was perhaps Lester Young's most lasting legacy, and it informs the playing of Getz's whole generation. This does not, however, mean that they simply copied Lester's methods. He worked in the comparatively simple, harmonically stable idiom of swing, whereas they were of the bebop generation and at home with a denser, more chromatic vocabulary, in which the sense of key is more fluid. In Getz's ballad playing this difference shows itself most clearly in the little linking passages between the main phrases of a tune. A good example occurs in 'Stars Fell On Alabama', from the December 12th session. He plays the first six bars of the theme virtually unaltered, with a plaintiveness that only Lester himself could have surpassed, but in the two 'empty' bars that follow he inserts a phrase based on a chromatic substitution – a quotation, in fact, from Dizzy Gillespie – which is pure bebop (in the key of C: Ebm7, Ab7 / Dm7, G7).

Although he had signed with Granz, Getz still owed Roost one session under his previous contract. This was recorded a week later, on December 19th, but to avoid any unpleasantness Roost attached the false date of December 5th to the documentation. This little subterfuge was to cause endless confusion among discographers in later years. The final Roost session resulted in four excellent performances – three ballads and a swinging version of George Shearing's 'Lullaby Of Birdland' – all under three minutes in length. To complete its first album for Granz's Clef label, the quintet returned to the studio on December 29th and recorded a further three ballads and a Gigi Gryce composition, 'Hymn Of The Orient'. Among the ballads is perhaps the only jazz version of 'Thanks For The Memory', Bob Hope's theme song.

The Clef album, containing all 12 numbers from the December sessions, came out in 1953, under the title *Stan Getz Plays*, but by that time Raney had left for the drug-free environment of vibraphonist Red Norvo's trio and the quintet was no more. Getz and Raney did, however, record together once more. It was for the Prestige label, in April 1953, in a quintet under Raney's leadership. In a token attempt at concealment, which fooled no one, Getz had himself billed as 'Sven Coolson'.

The four longish numbers – three Raney originals and Thelonious Monk's 'Round Midnight' – were released on a ten-inch LP entitled *Jimmy Raney Plays*. The pianist on this session is Hall Overton, the composer who was later to work with Monk on producing a set of glorious orchestral expansions of Monk's small-band music. The bassist is Red Mitchell and the drummer Frank Isola. Raney's themes are abstract, slightly tricky constructions, very much of their period, but the more generous playing time allows both Getz and Raney to stretch out and they play with all the spirit and empathy of their early partnership. This is particularly so in the piece entitled 'Motion', based on the changes of 'You Stepped Out Of A Dream', which prompts one to speculate on how much they might have achieved together had their relationship not become poisoned.

NEW SOUNDS

After the departure of Raney, Getz spent the early months of 1953 without a band. Since he was working in and around New York, he had no difficulty in finding musicians to make up temporary groups, but for touring he would need a fixed band, signed up in the regular way. He decided on another quintet, with valve-trombonist Bob Brookmeyer filling Raney's front-line position and a young pianist from Charlie

Barnet's orchestra, John Williams. Initially the bass and drums were Bill Crow and Al Levitt, later replaced by Teddy Kotick and Frank Isola.

The valve trombone is not a common instrument. As its name suggests, it has the pitch and general tone quality of the trombone, but the notes are produced not by means of a slide but with trumpet-type valves. It was quite popular with marching bands in the late 19th and early 20th centuries. Its jazz credentials are slim but venerable, since it was a feature of Buddy Bolden's band in New Orleans, often cited as the first-ever jazz band. Indeed, a valve trombone appears in the only known photograph of Bolden's band, in the hands of its player, Willie Cornish. Before Brookmeyer, the only other valve-trombonist of note in jazz had been Juan Tizol, who played it in the orchestras of Duke Ellington and Harry James. It is probably the easiest of all brass instruments to master, in a rudimentary way, but its natural sound is rather lifeless and inexpressive. In the hands of unwary jazz soloists it has a tendency to burble on like a company chairman delivering the annual report to shareholders. Even Brookmeyer himself is not entirely free of this, but in his case it is happy, good-natured burbling.

Brookmeyer, in any case, was and is a superb musician of broad accomplishments. Prior to joining Getz, most of his professional experience had been as a pianist and arranger (he was playing piano with Tex Beneke when Getz approached him), and Getz at once commissioned him to write material for the new quintet. Three of these numbers, 'Cool Mix', 'Rustic Hop' and 'Erudition', were recorded at the quintet's debut session, on May 16th 1953. 'Rustic Hop' – open, sunny and catchy – is a quintessential Brookmeyer theme. It is voiced in two independent parts, playfully tumbling and chasing one another, and this spirit is maintained through the whole piece, with Getz and Brookmeyer joining in with riffs behind each other's solos. Williams, although he takes no solo here and is slightly under-recorded, has exactly the right lively and ebullient style to suit the new partnership. 'Rustic Hop' runs for only three minutes and 45 seconds, near the extreme limit for a single 78 or 45, but it has the feeling of a complete, rounded performance and is the kind of bright, optimistic jazz that almost anyone can understand and enjoy.

Immediately after this session, the quintet played a week at the Blue Mirror in Washington DC and then left for California, where they were booked to appear at the Tiffany Club, Los Angeles. They were at the Tiffany at the same time that the Gerry Mulligan Quartet, with Chet Baker, was at the Haig club. "The Tiffany and the Haig were only about 10 or 12 blocks apart," recalled John Williams, "so every intermission we'd run out to the car, head for the Haig and hope we would hit it while they were playing. We'd listen to the band for about 20 minutes or so, and then back to the Tiffany. Chet and Gerry would do the same thing in reverse."[5]

At that precise moment, the Mulligan Quartet was the sensation of the jazz world. Its instrumentation of baritone saxophone, trumpet, bass and drums created a completely new sound, mainly because it contained no piano or other chordal instrument. The effect was uniquely delicate, and its attraction was enhanced by Mulligan's nimble playing of an instrument hitherto regarded as stately and a little ponderous, by Baker's sparkling, lyrical trumpet, and especially by Mulligan's simple, witty arrangements. However, along with his burgeoning celebrity, Mulligan, too, was a heroin addict. In an attempt to cure himself, he took time off from the Haig and retired to Palm Springs. Getz, whose Tiffany Club engagement had just finished, briefly filled in for him, and at one session the proceedings were recorded. The recordings, not officially released until both Getz and Baker were dead, make a fascinating addendum to the work of both men. Individually, they play beautifully, but there is none of the semi-humorous interplay that's such a feature of the Mulligan-Baker partnership. The plain fact is that Getz and Baker disliked each other on sight and maintained the wariest of relationships for the rest of their lives.

With plenty of work lined up in California, both for the quintet and as a star soloist with Granz's Jazz At The Philharmonic, Getz decided to bring his family out to join him on the West Coast. It was here, in a rented house in Laurel Canyon, that Beverly, his third child and first daughter, would be born.

ZARDI'S

The summer of 1953 was the quintet's most stable and productive period. For much of the time it was resident at Zardi's, on Hollywood Boulevard, which seems to have been the ideal club for a band like the Getz quintet. Pianist Lou Levy, who played there often, with Getz and others, remembered it with great affection: "It was a charming place to play. They had the bar there when you walked in and bamboo stools with red leather on top, a real South Pacific look... It didn't hold very many people. You might get in 200 customers if you broke the fire laws. It was very comfortable and we enjoyed playing there."[6]

Most owners of small, successful clubs sooner or later conceive the ambition of owning large, successful clubs, and Zardi's Ben Arkin was no exception. But it's a truth universally acknowledged among jazz musicians that when the boss starts talking about his plans for expanding and smartening up the premises, the writing is on the wall. And so it proved. Arkin enlarged and tarted up Zardi's, the magic evaporated, and by the end of 1957 the club was offering dining and dancing to Don Tosti's rumba band, plus a floorshow.

This sad tale highlights one of the problems that surfaced as jazz grew in popularity through the 1950s, namely that small-band jazz works best in intimate surroundings, but you can't provide intimacy to a mass audience. Nor can you afford to pay an artist like Stan Getz what he is worth when you can only get 200 people into your club, and even that is breaking the fire regulations. Getz played Zardi's six nights a week for seven weeks, to capacity crowds, but it brought him no more than a reasonable middle-class income. The problem persists to this day. The tenor saxophonist Scott Hamilton once mused that, if he were a novelist, and as many people bought his books as came to jazz clubs to hear him play, he would almost certainly be a millionaire.[7]

That summer, the quintet recorded three sessions for Granz (on July 30th and August 15th and 22nd), the results being released on two albums, *Interpretations* and *Interpretations 2*. Compared with the work of the previous band, with Jimmy Raney, the general impression is of something warmer, simpler, perhaps superficially less brilliant but immensely attractive nonetheless. Undoubtedly the catalyst for this change was Bob Brookmeyer. A native of Kansas City, who revered Count Basie and all the musical values he represented, Brookmeyer's penchant for genial, uncomplicated, swinging jazz was obvious from the start.

Another important ingredient is John Williams's piano, especially his work in the rhythm section. Stylistically, he falls about halfway between Al Haig and Horace Silver, with his rumbling, muttering left-hand figures and sharp interjections. He generates a nervous energy which provides the perfect complement to Brookmeyer's unbuttoned ease.

The very first number recorded, a version of Irving Berlin's 'Love And The Weather', sums up all these qualities. Taken at a sauntering 48 bars a minute, with Brookmeyer and Getz taking turns with the lead in the theme statements, and Williams dodging around them like an unleashed puppy, it reveals Getz at his most mellow and buoyant. Here, you might think, is the voice of a truly happy and well-adjusted man. The same is true of the lively 'Crazy Rhythm', energetically stoked throughout by Williams and featuring a wildly free-associating Getz solo. Getz and Brookmeyer developed a remarkable rapport, which enabled them to play long passages together without getting tied up in knots. Very often it's impossible to tell where Brookmeyer's written arrangement leaves off and the improvisation starts. The slow ballad 'The Nearness Of You' is a case in point. The whole number, apart from an eight-bar piano interlude, is played by Getz and Brookmeyer as a duet. The opening few bars are obviously written, but thereafter the two lines cross so cleverly and dissonances resolve so neatly that the transition is impossible to locate.

Now that 12-inch long-playing records were becoming established, Norman Granz had adopted the practice of recording all-star studio jam sessions along the lines of his JATP concerts. Getz took part in one on August 3rd, featuring, among others, Count Basie, trumpeter Harry 'Sweets' Edison, clarinettist Buddy DeFranco, alto saxophonists Benny Carter and Willie Smith, and Wardell Gray as the other tenor. The four long tracks consist mainly of opening and closing themes separated by a string of solos, which, given the cast involved, could hardly be less than enjoyable. The main interest here, however, is the comparison between Getz and Wardell Gray, one of the few tenor players he admired unreservedly. Their two styles derived initially from the same sources, Lester Young and bebop, but they had developed in opposite directions. Gray's clear, bright, almost severe tone was matched by an improvised line of such sculptural purity that expressive devices of any kind would have been out of place. He negotiated the chromatic intricacies of bebop with spare, athletic grace and a burning intelligence that can bring tears to the eyes. He was the greatest of all bebop tenor saxophonists and his untimely death in May 1955 is a cause of infinite regret. To hear Gray and Getz together is to be reminded of the infinite variety of which jazz music is capable, even among musicians of the same generation.

CHAPTER 7

Everything
Happens to Me

"Tell this boy in Seattle that it's pure and simple degeneracy of the mind, a lack of morals and personality shortcomings I have and he doesn't."

STAN GETZ ANSWERING A 1954 JAZZ MAGAZINE

LETTER DENOUNCING DOPE ADDICTS

A band without a gig soon ceases to exist. The Zardi's residency drew to a close in September 1953 with no further quintet work in sight. Getz took up the offer of a tour as star guest soloist with his old boss Stan Kenton, and the others gradually drifted off wherever freelance work took them, in the vague hope that they might all get together again should something turn up.

Getz returned from the Kenton tour in October and played casually around Los Angeles for a while. An offer came in for the quintet to play the first week in December at the Hi-Hat club in Boston. He managed to round up Brookmeyer and Kotick, but not the other two, whose places he filled with Duke Jordan and Roy Haynes. On December 9th he flew back to Los Angeles and straight into one of the most demanding recording sessions of his life, for which Granz had paired him with Dizzy Gillespie, accompanied by the Oscar Peterson trio, plus Max Roach on drums.

It is fascinating to listen to the eight numbers constituting *Diz And Getz* in the order they were recorded – in this case not the order in which they appear on the vinyl album and subsequent CD release. According

Getz on-stage with Tony Fruscella, who joined the quintet after Bob Brookmeyer left

to the tape master numbers allocated at the session, the first piece was the easy-going 'Girl Of My Dreams', in which both principals sound a little wary of one another. Getz, in particular, is uncharacteristically tentative, almost shy. Next comes Ellington's 'It Don't Mean A Thing (If It Ain't Got That Swing)' taken at the crazy pace of 84 bars a minute. At that speed it doesn't actually swing at all, but drives like fury, and Getz matches Gillespie's tumbling ebullience up to and including the four-bar exchanges following Roach's climactic drum solo.

Having survived these preliminary skirmishes, everyone relaxes into the ballad 'It's The Talk Of The Town', but only, one suspects, after some lively exchanges on the subject of key, because this is, to all intents and purposes, two performances – Dizzy's two choruses in F and, following a four-bar piano modulation, two more from Getz in A-flat. He would have been intent on sounding his best in a ballad, and A-flat was the key in which his gorgeous middle register would have its full impact.

There are two versions of the next number, too, the Latin-American standard 'Siboney'. Getz does not play at all on the first, but leads most of the way on the second. For the first, Gillespie sticks to the minor-key section of the song, which he treats in the traditional Cuban way as a montuno, or single chord. Getz, on the other hand, alternates between the major and minor sections, thus providing himself with some changes to get a grip on. The next two pieces, 'Exactly Like You' and 'I Let A Song Go Out Of My Heart', provide the best music of the whole session, with both soloists luxuriating in the wonderful, rolling swing generated by Peterson and the rhythm section. The final number, Gillespie's own 'Impromptu', goes quite well but both he and Getz sound as though they have had enough.

What this session seems to tell us about Getz is that he played to his strengths, insisted on tackling given material in his own way, and tried always to make sure he was heard to his best advantage. It also suggests that what is presented to the public as a happy-go-lucky jam session is not necessarily anything of the sort.

Getz returned to Zardi's for the week leading up to Christmas 1953, sharing the spotlight with Chet Baker and accompanied by a rhythm section led by pianist Jimmy Rowles. The Los Angeles Police Department had been keeping an eye on him for some time, but Getz was an experienced drug user. He never carried with him his 'works', or drug-taking equipment, but stashed it away under stones or among bushes at the roadside. Normally he injected himself in the rest-rooms of service stations and suchlike anonymous places. He could not, however, ensure that Beverly was as circumspect as he was, nor could he disguise the needle-marks on his arms. He had just returned home in the early hours of December 19th when three policemen, led by an officer with the entirely plausible name of Detective O'Grady, forced their way into his house. There followed a depressingly familiar series of events: Getz panicked, waved a handgun around and then, fortunately, dropped it. Beverly was observed flushing a package down the toilet. The officers rolled up Getz's sleeve, noted the marks and booked him on the curious charge of vagrancy and drug addiction.

The whole sorry episode was summed up in a single newspaper headline: 'Top Jazz Musician Nabbed in Dope Raid on Hollywood Home – Needle Marks on Arm Told'.[1] Getz was bailed and his trial took place a month later. He pleaded guilty and was ordered to return for sentencing a month later still. In one respect he was lucky. The police decided not to press charges of resisting arrest with a gun, which they might easily have done, and they overlooked Beverly's flushing away of evidence, which could also have led to further charges.

In the middle of all this (two days after his court appearance, in fact), Getz recorded four three-minute numbers with Rowles, Roach and bassist Bob Whitlock, which sound as blithe and untroubled as a May morning. 'Nobody Else But Me', 'With The Wind And The Rain In Your Hair', 'I Hadn't Anyone But You' and 'Down By The Sycamore Tree' are performances as serene as any he ever recorded. They stand as a powerful caution to anyone tempted to read a musician's autobiography in his music. It all depends on the musician. Getz, it seems, stepped into a whole different world when he picked up his instrument, a world of order and light and softly breathing passion. By contrast, Lester Young's playing unfailingly betrayed his day-to-day feelings, his state of health, his forebodings, his whimsical passing thoughts and gently ironical cast of mind.

DRUGLESS IN SEATTLE

Getz was due to be sentenced on February 17th 1954. On the 5th he embarked on a short West Coast concert tour with a package show assembled by promoter Gene Norman. Facing a drugless 90-day sentence, and believing he was now a marked man, he decided to kick the heroin habit while on tour, with the aid of barbiturates and alcohol. He would have done better to check into a clinic and come down under expert supervision. The withdrawal symptoms became intolerable and his mood swings alienated everyone else on the tour. By the time they reached Seattle, early in the morning on the fifth day, he had become completely manic and disoriented. Across the street from his hotel was a drugstore. He walked in, stuck his hand in his jacket pocket, pretending it was a gun, and demanded morphine. He can't have made a very convincing job of it, because the woman behind the counter demanded to see the gun first. Another customer looked at him, laughed and said, "Lady, he's kidding. He has no gun." Whereupon the amateur stick-up man fled.

Back in his hotel room, he looked up the phone number of the drugstore, called it and apologised to the counter clerk. By this time there were two policemen in the store, taking statements. One of them, pretending to be a doctor, took the phone and offered to help. Getz told him the hotel and room number and then, in an apparent suicide attempt, took 60 grains of long-acting barbiturate. The police found him wandering the hotel corridors, arrested and handcuffed him, bundled him into a squad-car, took him downtown, booked him, and dumped him in a cell. By now the barbiturates were taking effect. Half an hour later he was found unconscious and close to death. He was rushed to hospital, an emergency tracheotomy performed and a tube inserted in his windpipe. He lay unconscious for three days.

The whole episode was a gift to the press: 'Crazed by Dope: Noted Musician Collapses in Jail After Hold-up Attempt'.[2] There were pictures of his arrest and tearful interviews with reporters, full of self-loathing and promises to reform. Once again he was lucky to be booked only on the charge of habitual narcotics use, not for attempted robbery. He was released on $1,500 bail and bound over to return to Seattle to face charges after serving his sentence in Los Angeles. He then left for LA to face the judge.

And the judge really let him have it, calling him, "a poor excuse for a man" and pointing out the undeniable facts that he had betrayed his talent, disgraced his parents and failed to take proper care of his family. What the judge could not know was that, on this last count, Beverly was the worse offender of the two. "Despite an income of a thousand dollars a week," he thundered, "you are not only broke but your family is living under deplorable conditions. They are sleeping on the floor while you travel in luxury."[3] Someone had obviously taken a look around chez Getz in Laurel Canyon and noted that it wasn't exactly the ideal all-American home. Stan himself was almost compulsively neat and tidy, in both his personal appearance and his immediate surroundings, but he was the product of a culture in which men went out to work and women kept the home, raised the children and administered chicken soup of legendary efficacy. His own mother, Goldie, had been a Jewish matriarch on this pattern, even though sorely tried by her husband's passivity and incompetence, and one may suppose that Getz assumed his wife would fill a similar role. But Beverly had not been raised in a traditional Jewish family. Her parents were vaudeville entertainers who were constantly on tour and she had more or less brought herself up, under the wing of her street-wise big brother Buddy, who was now dead. The word 'home' probably had very little meaning for her. What's more, she was high as a kite most of the time.

So the place was a squalid mess and the judge blamed Stan for it. Instead of the expected 90 days, he handed down 180, plus three years' probation. When the severity of the sentence was relayed to the court in Seattle, the authorities there decided not to proceed with the charges arising from the drug store episode back in February, which must have caused some relief. With Stan in the county jail and no money coming in, Beverly sold off what was left of the furniture. When it was gone, the money spent and the electricity cut off, she threw herself and her three kids on Norman Granz's mercy. Granz arranged for her to receive a weekly allowance for the duration of Stan's sentence.

From the county jail, Getz was moved to a low-security prison-farm in the San Fernando Valley – they recognised that he posed more danger to himself than to other people. It was from here that he wrote his now-famous letter to the editor of *Down Beat*, in answer to a young would-be musician who had written expressing horror at the thought of one day "playing next to a dope addict". In his response Getz recounts the Seattle episode and concludes that "God didn't want to kill me", although the almighty may not take such a lenient view in the future. He had been heartened by messages from lovers of his music, saying they were praying for him, "that I should pray as they were praying for me, and, most important, that they forgave me." After more in this religiose vein there comes the following extraordinary sentence: "Tell this boy in Seattle that it's pure and simple degeneracy of the mind, a lack of morals and personality shortcomings I have and he doesn't."[4]

These traits of which he accuses himself are all presented as innate, fixed and irremovable. The Christian equivalent would be to say he believed himself damned. Did he really believe this, that he was so hopelessly wicked that there was no help for him in this world? If so, it may point to the cause of the self-destructive rages which were to surface so alarmingly in his later life. These were sometimes attributed to 'depression', but 'despair' might be a better word. It was, of course, a punitive and unforgiving era, in which any form of drug-taking was harshly condemned and savagely punished. Perhaps Getz internalised these judgments and applied them to himself.

AT THE SHRINE

He was released in August 1954 and went straight back to work, joining Chet Baker at the Tiffany Club. One can think of safer company for a newly released and drug-free heroin offender, but he could not wait to get back on the bandstand. This was followed by a return to Zardi's, and then came a chance to re-form his quintet with Brookmeyer. This was for a concert tour organised by Norman Granz, also featuring Duke Ellington & His Famous Orchestra, the Dave Brubeck Quartet and the Gerry Mulligan Quartet. This time he managed to get hold of John Williams from the original band, but the bass and drums were Bill Anthony and Art Mardigan.

The tour played to full houses, including Carnegie Hall, throughout October, finishing at the Shrine Auditorium in Los Angeles on November 8th. Here the quintet's segment was recorded by Granz and later released as an album entitled *Stan Getz At The Shrine*. Among the record's peripheral interests are Getz's announcements. Hearing his eager, boyish voice it is easy to understand how he had managed to talk himself out of several tight corners with the police by acting the innocent novice, led astray by bad company. With his baby face and candid, wide-eyed stare, he also looked the part.

But to return to the music: it's clear from the looseness and ease of its performance that here is a band that is played-in and at the peak of its form. After the opening 'Flamingo', Getz disarmingly says to the audience, "I hope you recognised it. We almost lost it a few times..." In fact, no confusion is discernible, here or anywhere else. The interplay between Getz and Brookmeyer is quite remarkable, two minds in perfect accord, moving with complete freedom yet never at cross-purposes. Once again it is difficult to tell where arrangement ends and improvisation begins, particularly in slow ballads – the opening of 'Loverman' is a particularly good example. Most of the numbers end with quite long improvised codas by the two of them, full of humour, surprise and delight. *Stan Getz At The Shrine* made a great impression when it came out, and it remains one of the most popular albums among Getz lovers to this day. Its combination of abundant imagination, high spirits and effortless virtuosity has proved irresistible for almost half a century. Nothing could illustrate this better than a comparison between the version of 'It Don't Mean A Thing' with which the Shrine concert ends and the one on *Diz And Getz*. The latter is quite transparently a contest, a trial of strength and velocity, whereas the Shrine performance, at a more sensible 72 bars a minute, is more like a celebration.

On the day following the Shrine concert, Granz recorded a studio session by the quintet, this time with Frank Isola back in the drum chair. The atmosphere is different, of course, but the music equally delightful, especially 'Give Me The Simple Life' and a casual-sounding version of an old Basie blues, 'Feather Merchant'. This begins with several choruses of typical, spiky John Williams piano before Getz and

Brookmeyer come in. Sadly, this session marks the end of the regular Getz-Brookmeyer partnership, although they did get together again from time to time. In this instance the split was quite amicable. Brookmeyer had plans of his own.

In December, Getz played at Birdland's fifth anniversary celebration, as guest soloist with the Count Basie orchestra. The proceedings were recorded. Getz plays three numbers – Neal Hefti's 'Little Pony', the ballad 'Easy Living' and 'Nails', a blues by Buster Harding. 'Little Pony' had originally been Wardell Gray's feature number when he was a member of Basie's band. His is the definitive recording, and it is plain that Getz can't quite shake off the Gray influence, although he tries valiantly. He is much more himself on the other two titles. He was later to tour with Basie in the package show *Birdland Stars Of 1955*.

If he was to continue with a quintet, Getz needed to find a replacement for Brookmeyer. He settled on Tony Fruscella, a trumpet player virtually unknown to the jazz public but with a growing underground reputation among musicians. Fruscella was a lyrical player, somewhat in the Chet Baker mould, with a delicate tone and resourceful imagination. The problem, as John Williams put it, was that, "Tony was hardly in this world. He was a sweet guy with the most incredible creative talents, but it was difficult for him to function in the real world."[5] In fact Fruscella, who had been brought up in an orphanage, was virtually a vagrant. He rarely had a fixed address and almost never a telephone number. He carried his trumpet around in a brown paper bag. Very little survives of Fruscella's couple of months with the quintet. There are some fragments of a jam session unofficially recorded in Washington DC in December 1954, three numbers culled from a Birdland broadcast on January 23rd 1955, and two pieces recorded by Granz on January 31st. These suggest that, from the musical point of view, theirs could have been a promising partnership, but with two people as unstable as Getz and Fruscella it was doomed. Shortly after the studio session they came to blows and Fruscella left.

FALLING OFF A LOG

Getz's work was now increasingly taking him to New York and the east coast. It made sense, therefore, to move his family back there. In February he was booked to play a series of dates across the country with Basie in the Birdland Stars package tour. He arranged for Beverly and the children to travel by car with a friend to Kansas City, where he would meet them and drive to New York. The car ran off the road near Stroud, Oklahoma, crashing into a bridge support. All except the baby, Beverly Patricia, were seriously injured. Three-year-old David Getz and the driver, Tom Killough, were not expected to survive; Beverly had a fractured spine; eldest son Steve had concussion and a broken arm. Killough died without regaining consciousness, but the Getz family eventually recovered. In the cases of Beverly and David the recovery period was prolonged and difficult.

On March 14th Getz took part in an unusual session under the auspices of a body called the Modern Jazz Society, organised by Gunther Schuller and John Lewis. Schuller, who had played French horn on Miles Davis's *Birth Of The Cool* recordings, was at the time a member of the Metropolitan Opera House orchestra. Lewis was musical director and pianist of the successful Modern Jazz Quartet, who were interested in creating a fusion of European classical music and jazz, an amalgam which would later be labelled 'Third Stream Music'. Getz's contribution to the recording consists of solos on 'The Queen's Fancy' by Lewis, and Schuller's 'Midsommer'. Getz was always ready to try something new if it promised to be interesting, and in this instance his tenor saxophone blends remarkably well with the unusual tone-colours, especially in the dreamy 'Midsommer'.

Stan Getz could be utterly charming when he chose, and he was notorious among musicians for making a pass at any reasonably presentable woman who crossed his path. As though his life were not complicated enough already, in this respect it often resembled a French farce. He was forever devising stratagems to keep one temporary girlfriend from finding out about the others. However, he had met a young Swedish student in Washington DC, while on the Birdland tour, who had seriously captivated him. Chicks were chicks and broads were broads, but Monica Silfverskiold was a different class of being altogether. She was a child of the Swedish aristocracy, daughter of a distinguished surgeon and granddaughter of Count Eric von Rosen. Educated, high-minded, socially poised, non-smoking, teetotal, Monica was everything that Beverly was not. She was also impossibly beautiful, in a Grace Kelly-ish kind of way. Getz resolved to put an end to his marriage, with all its attendant squalor, and seek a new life with Monica.

Having removed from Los Angeles to New York, and with his wife and younger son still recuperating there from the accident, Getz now found himself back on the west coast. The cause was the filming of *The Benny Goodman Story*, for which he was to be a member of the on-screen band and play on the soundtrack recording. The movie had been hastily set up to capitalise on the recent huge success of *The Glenn Miller Story*, in which James Stewart had portrayed the notoriously frosty Miller as a determined but fundamentally amiable individual. Goodman, as played by Steve Allen, came across as virtually devoid of any character or personality at all. Some cynics viewed this as a distinct improvement on the real thing. Getz's contract required him to be available throughout July and August 1955, although much of that time would inevitably be spent doing nothing. During the idle hours he took to calling at the home of bassist Leroy Vinnegar, where he would often jam with Vinnegar, pianist Lou Levy and drummer Shelly Manne. This quartet soon had a two-week booking at Zardi's. Norman Granz also decided to make use of Getz's unexpected presence in Hollywood to set up another double-headed session, this time with Lionel Hampton, who was featuring in the Goodman film and also at a loose end. Getz brought the rest of the Zardi's quartet along to form the rhythm section.

The album *Hamp And Getz* has none of the initial awkwardness of the earlier Gillespie session and radiates good feeling from start to finish. Even at 80 bars a minute, the opening number, the formidable 'Cherokee', sounds like a romp. Because he was an extrovert and a dedicated showman, Hampton's remarkable powers as an improviser have often been overlooked. He shared with Getz the ability to give himself up completely to the music, becoming lost in patterns of sound and oblivious to the world when he was playing. He also had a habit of mumbling and chuckling to himself while doing so, which is much in evidence here. 'Cherokee' finds Getz at his most robust and forthright, interspersing clean, hard-edged phrases with smears and wailing blues figures. 'Louise', by contrast, is disarmingly sweet and simple. Getz and Hampton stay close to the melody throughout, matched by Lou Levy's unadorned harmonies. The 'ballad medley' had become a regular feature of Granz productions by now, both live and on record. Getz's choices this time were 'Tenderly' and 'Autumn In New York', immaculately played, but not exceptional by his standards. 'Jumpin' At The Woodside', on the other hand, is inspired. Getz opens his solo with a number of direct references to Lester Young, whose solo on the original 1938 Basie record he probably knew by heart. The number reaches its climax through a series of exchanges between Getz and Hampton, first eight bars each, then four and gradually closing in on each other until they are both going simultaneously at full stretch, with occasional shouts from Hampton adding to the general excitement.

The actual soundtrack recordings from *The Benny Goodman Story* are quite good, although Getz plays only a few brief solos. From his point of view the real action was taking place with the Levy-Vinnegar-Manne team at Zardi's and at Norman Granz's recording sessions. On August 15th, the quartet, plus trumpeter Conte Candoli, recorded seven numbers for an album which would eventually be released as *West Coast Jazz*. The title was intended as a mild joke, the point of which was to make fun of the supposed east-west dichotomy in jazz at the time. West-coast jazz was characterised as refined and cerebral, while east-coast jazz was full-blooded and robust. None of the participants at the session was a native Californian, and the three jazz compositions included were of impeccable east-coast origin, namely Miles Davis's 'Four', Horace Silver's 'Split Kick' and Dizzy Gillespie's 'A Night In Tunisia'. None of this matters now. The important point about *West Coast Jazz* is that it includes a Getz solo of such brilliance that it would, on its own, qualify him for a place among the great jazz musicians.

The number in question is 'Shine', an ancient vaudeville number by Cecil Mack and Lew Brown, dating from 1924. Goodman played it occasionally, and included it in the soundtrack album of *The Benny Goodman Story*, and Louis Armstrong played and sang it in the 1942 movie *Cabin In The Sky*, but no 'modern' jazz musician ever seems to have thought of it. The performance begins with an unaccompanied eight-bar introduction by Getz. This constitutes a technical tour de force on its own account, the first four bars consisting of a string of even, soft-tongued quavers (eighth-notes) in repeated pairs. The audacity of the idea and the utter perfection of its realisation sum up the technical mastery which, even today, makes Getz the despair of other saxophonists. This is followed by no fewer than 18 choruses of concentrated invention, at once passionate and logical, produced with a kind of silky insouciance.

For speed and continuity of thought (at a tempo of around 74 bars a minute), rhythmic poise, fertility of imagination and sheer completeness as a musical utterance, the 'Shine' solo can only be compared with Lester Young's recording debut, almost 20 years earlier. Everything about it is enthralling, and it retains its power to astound the listener after endlessly repeated playings. As in the case of Lester Young's 'Lady Be Good', the task of following the tenor saxophone falls to the hapless trumpet player. For the rest of his life, Conte Candoli bore the condolences of history with a rueful good grace. Getz, when asked about the 'Shine' solo by the English writer Steve Voce, replied that it was done in one take and had been "as easy as falling off a log". Some log.

The *West Coast Jazz* recording was followed four days later by a quartet session that yielded four elegant ballad performances, later issued as part of the album *Stan Getz & The Cool Sounds*. In 1996 a complete set of Getz's mid-1950s recordings with Lou Levy was issued, including false starts, breakdowns and a certain amount of studio conversation. Some numbers, notably 'Shine', go straight through in one take, while others give trouble. One of these is the Gershwin tune 'Of Thee I Sing', from the second session, which begins no fewer than eight times, with the voice of engineer Val Valentin intoning the master and take numbers in-between. Some starts result in complete takes, some break down and some barely get started. But despite these frustrations, the atmosphere throughout is notably calm and businesslike. One cannot help being struck, too, by the utter dependability of Vinnegar's bass, with its resonant tone, immaculate choice of notes and rock-steady time.

The Goodman movie was completed at around the time of these sessions, and the Zardi's gig had come to an end. Getz's heroin habit was firmly back in place too – all his good resolutions forgotten or thrust into a dark corner. He returned to New York but, perhaps to avoid confronting his bedridden wife, his neglected children and his despairing and bewildered parents, he bolted to the one place that had nothing but happy associations for him. He bought an airline ticket to Stockholm.

CHAPTER 8

Ghost of
a Chance

"The horn was an expression of his head. There were no barriers. The music just came rolling out."

DRUMMER STAN LEVEY, WHO PLAYED OFTEN WITH GETZ IN THE 1950s, ON THE MAN'S INSTRUMENTAL PROWESS

He arrived in Sweden, unannounced save for a cable dispatched to Monica *en route*, deep in the throes of withdrawal and with no idea where his next fix might come from. One can only imagine the thoughts of Monica's genteel family as this apparition came lurching into their lives. He contrived to find a heroin connection and calmed down, but a few days later he collapsed with a combination of pneumonia and pleurisy and almost died.

The hospital had to give him morphine to relieve the withdrawal symptoms, but when the worst of the infection was over they began reducing the dose, whereupon he became so violent that he had to be confined in a straightjacket. Despite this alarming introduction to his lifestyle, Monica decided that she had fallen in love with him.

Once he was out of hospital and reasonably stable, Getz recorded a session for the Swedish Karusell label, which had contractual links with Norman Granz. He seems a little subdued and, with the gentle Bengt Hallberg on piano, the outcome sounds rather like a throwback to his early 'watercolour' period.

Getz and Frank Isola, mid-1950s

Stan Getz NOBODY ELSE BUT ME

Perhaps the most interesting of the eight numbers is a curious version of 'Get Happy', reworked in a minor key. Interviewed by Nat Hentoff for the notes to the resulting album, *Stan Getz In Stockholm*, Getz remarked: "There are times when I feel that Bengt borders on genius ... He has a beautiful soul for music; I can hear it when he plays. I've known and listened to him since 1950. He has ambivalent feelings about jazz, though. He doesn't like the uncertainty of it, and thinks it's a limited form ... He doesn't permit himself to get excited when he plays jazz. He's afraid of letting himself go that much; he's afraid he'll get hurt. And yet I know he could Bud-Powell it up if he wanted to."

Can this astute and sympathetic observation have come from a man who, a couple of months earlier, had been behaving so violently as to require physical restraint? The answer is yes, and there was more to come. As Zoot Sims once famously declared: "Stan Getz? A nice bunch of guys."

The medical advice was that Getz should not attempt to resume his performing career for a while, although he could practise, to strengthen his lungs. It was decided that he and Monica should take a holiday in Kenya. All went well at first, until he got hold of some barbiturates, mixed them with alcohol, went out of his head and cut Monica's clothes to shreds with a razor. As usual, he apologised abjectly and profusely when the effects had worn off, only to do the same again. This time he attacked her, after first smashing up his saxophone. He was locked up in the local police station and eventually released on the intervention of the Swedish ambassador. The couple returned to Sweden, having first cooked up a story about a car crash, to explain why Monica's face was covered in bruises and plaster.

Getz began playing again in the spring of 1956 and in September he joined a month-long JATP tour, which also featured the Modern Jazz Quartet, Dizzy Gillespie and Sonny Stitt. A saxophonist of phenomenal dexterity and drive, Stitt was a master of the bebop idiom. When he played alto he was obviously deep in Parker's shadow, although his phrasing tended to be more squarely centred within the bar-lines. He played with greater individuality on tenor, but his alto was the more spectacular. He was also one of the most aggressively competitive musicians in jazz.

Getz liked to tell a story about Sonny Stitt and Lester Young aboard a JATP tour bus. Lester was relaxing, his hat tipped over his eyes. "Stitt took out his horn and began walking up and down the aisle playing all his licks. Nobody paid any attention to him," recounted Getz, "so he finally went over to Lester and said, 'Hey, Pres, whaddya think of that?' Pres, his eyes half closed, said, 'Yes, Lady Stitt, but can you sing me a song?'."[1]

At the end of the tour, Norman Granz brought Gillespie, Stitt and Getz into the studio and the four long pieces recorded on October 16th, issued under the title *For Musicians Only*, capture very well not only Stitt's ferocity but the way his presence was able to galvanise everyone else. At tempos of around 86 and 84 bars a minute respectively, Gillespie's 'Bebop' and Denzil Best's 'Wee' (also known as 'Allen's Alley') have something of the rodeo about them, the immediate aim being to stay in the saddle, however inelegantly. Certainly Getz's solos display none of the qualities for which he is most admired, expressiveness being the first casualty of extreme speed, but he matches Stitt and Gillespie. The other two numbers, 'Dark Eyes' and 'Lover Come Back To Me', are a little more moderate, but the whole enterprise illustrates the folly of trying to recreate the febrile excitement of a live show in the cold light of the morning after.

STANLEY THE STEAMER

There could be no greater contrast with the Stitt-Gillespie session than the following one, a month later, which found Getz reunited with Lou Levy and Leroy Vinnegar. This time, in place of Shelly Manne, the drummer was Stan Levey. It is obvious from the first few bars of the opening number, 'Blues For Mary Jane', that a subtle change has come about in Getz's playing. The tone is thicker, the phrasing almost severe in its simplicity and the approach altogether broader and more expansive. Like the previous year's 'Shine', the blues begins with an unaccompanied tenor introduction, followed by a long solo of formidable coherence. Each of the 12 choruses grows out of the one before and leads naturally into the next. The eighth and ninth are played in 'stop-time', in which the rhythm section marks only the first beat of the bar at two-bar intervals – in effect, a series of breaks. Returning after piano and bass solos, Getz plays a further seven choruses, the first of which is so melodic and symmetrical that it may well have been intended as the opening theme. The traditional blues form, the loping tempo (around 46 bars a minute), the use of stop-time (a venerable practice rarely employed by jazz musicians of his generation), the candid simplicity of the improvised line – all these add up to the impression that this is timeless music, unattached to any particular jazz fashion or movement or school.

The album, when it came out, was called *The Steamer*, apparently a reference to Oscar Peterson's nickname for Getz, 'Stanley The Steamer'. This time the six numbers appear in the order in which they were recorded. 'Blues For Mary Jane' was accomplished in a single take, as was the fourth, 'Too Close For Comfort'; presumably they both came into the 'falling off a log' category. The remaining four went through a variety of alternative takes, breakdowns and false starts, which are sometimes interesting for the light they throw on Getz's studio methods. For example, they work through two false starts before achieving a complete take of 'How About You?', but Getz is still not satisfied. He decides to change the introduction from eight bars of piano to eight bars of tenor, and thus, after one further false start, they arrive at the version included on the album.

Whatever personal difficulties may have arisen, almost everyone who ever worked with Stan Getz remarked on his qualities as a bandleader. Lou Levy claimed that he was "the best-organised musician I ever met. He knew how to play a tune from scratch, how to make up an ending. He had his shit together."[2] And, at around the time of this session, Leroy Vinnegar remarked, "He never gets in your way, and if he sets a tempo here it swings here." However disorganised he may have been in other respects, Getz was formidably systematic on stage, laying down exact procedures to be followed. "One of these," Vinnegar recalled, "was the three hand-signals he used to indicate which ending he wanted attached to a particular tune."[3]

The Steamer is a beautiful album in every respect – measured, mature, full of sweetness and controlled passion. One of its high points is the slow ballad 'You're Blasé', a 28-bar song by the British composer Ord Hamilton, dating from 1932. Getz habitually approached pieces like this very much as a singer might, holding close to the melody in the first chorus and expanding on it in the second, but always retaining the essential character of the song.

Rudolf Nureyev once said that true artistry resides not in making a complicated step look simple, but in making a simple step look interesting. Getz's simplicity fits this maxim precisely. To take one tiny example from 'You're Blasé': in the 14th bar of the tune there is a busy little harmonic movement in which the chords change with each beat, dropping a semitone at a time. Some players would seize on this, filling those four beats with a hail of notes and destroying the mood. Others would adopt different tactics. Getz's idea is simple elegance personified. He trails lazily down the notes of the major chord of the key, touching each of the descending chords at a different interval. (Assuming the key of F, the four chords are Eb, D7, Db7, C7, and Getz's notes are C, A, F, D – ie sixth, fifth, third, ninth.) It's only a passing moment, lasting about three seconds, and the description in words makes it seem far more complicated than it is. The point is that one could pick out a snatch of Getz almost at random and find something equally delightful and clever.

NO BARRIERS

Getz's divorce from Beverly came through and he and Monica were married in Las Vegas (where else?) on November 3rd 1956. With Swedish efficiency, Monica soon conducted a brisk examination of their financial position, only to be appalled by what she discovered. There were huge bills dating back to the time of the Oklahoma road accident and even before, demands from lawyers, hospitals, the California court officials (fines for not reporting to his probation officer) and, most ominous of all, the income tax authorities, the dreaded IRS.

As a bandleader, Getz had been acting as an employer. This meant that he was responsible for collecting his employees' taxes and passing them on to the IRS, which he had not done – or, rather, he had collected them but neglected to pass them on. Nor had he paid his own tax. Monica consulted yet more lawyers, who came to the inescapable conclusion that the Getzes were well and truly broke. He was declared bankrupt in March 1957, but the IRS still wanted their money. They obtained an order empowering them to collect a sizeable portion of his income as he earned it.

Getz put together a new quartet at the beginning of 1957, with yet another promising discovery, Mose Allison, as pianist and a bass-and-drums team that eventually settled down as Addison Farmer and Jerry Segal. This band lasted for about eight months, during which time they recorded one studio session. Fortunately, however, a fair amount of broadcast material survives. The great days of live radio broadcasts from clubs and ballrooms were long past, but the practice still continued on a reduced scale. The Getz quartet broadcast several times over the Mutual network, from the Red Hill Inn, in Pennsauken, New Jersey, and from New York's Village Vanguard. The sound quality of the off-air recording leaves something to be desired, but there are many good moments in the surviving fragments, including Getz's only known performance of 'Is It True What They Say About Dixie?' – not quite in the 'Shine' class, but impressive and high-spirited nonetheless. He had an endearing fondness for Dixieland music, dating from his days with Jack Teagarden, which he often cited as having been the best apprenticeship a young jazz musician could receive. "We'd play 'Struttin' With Some Barbecue' and 'That's A-Plenty'. I liked them, and I was in fact weaned on it. You should be able to play Dixieland. You don't have to, but you find it a big help."[4]

Allison proved to be a great asset. Not only was he a highly competent pianist, with a natural affinity for Getz's approach (at other times he played with both Zoot Sims and Al Cohn), he was then in the process of perfecting the unique style of singing, playing and songwriting which was to make his name. Born at Tippo, Mississippi, in the heart of blues country, he had fallen simultaneously under the spell of country blues and the emerging modern jazz movement. As a boy, his heroes had included both Sonny Boy Williamson and Nat King Cole. By 1957, he had developed an unmistakably original voice – guarded, gently sardonic, couched in the idiom of the down-home blues but spiced with knowing, metropolitan wit. In an unprecedented move, Getz would leave the stage to Allison for one number in each set, the single surviving broadcast example being 'Ain't You A Mess!', from one of the Red Hill dates.

The quartet's studio session, on July 12th, yielded five numbers for an album entitled *The Soft Swing*. They confirm that the changes evident in *The Steamer* were not temporary. 'All The Things You Are', one of many interpretations recorded by Getz over the years, is very fine, but perhaps the best piece is 'Bye Bye Blues', another Dixieland escapee. Taking it at a lively 70 bars a minute, Getz develops formidable impetus, partly through the use of a device much favoured by Lester Young, involving the rhythmic and tonal manipulation of a single note. By the use of alternative fingerings it is possible to create different densities of sound on certain notes. This, combined with varied attack and the right rhythmic phrasing, has the effect of raising the pressure and propelling the solo line forward. The practice was adopted and crudely employed by early rock saxophonists, but Lester Young and Stan Getz are the ones who brought it to its greatest pitch of subtlety.

During the life of this quartet, Getz continued to function as a member of Norman Granz's all-star repertory company. In June he took part in a studio jam session, alongside Dizzy Gillespie and two other tenor saxophonists, Coleman Hawkins and Paul Gonsalves. Like Lester Young, he rarely sounds comfortable in these circumstances, for reasons already discussed. Predictably, his best moments come during the two ballad medleys. In the first he plays 'Time After Time', a number from the repertoire of his current quartet, and in the second 'I'm Through With Love', of which this is his only released recording. Two years later it would be sung by Marilyn Monroe in the movie *Some Like It Hot*.

Mose Allison left in July, to follow up the success of his first solo album, *The Back Country Suite*. His departure, taking Addison Farmer with him, marked the end of the quartet and Getz left for Los Angeles to make two recording sessions. The first of these was an all-star date, rather better organised than usual, with Harry 'Sweets' Edison, Gerry Mulligan, the Oscar Peterson Trio and drummer Louie Bellson – released the following year as *Jazz Giants 58*. The next day, August 2nd 1957, saw the last of the Getz-Levy-Vinnegar sessions, with Stan Levey once more playing drums. Again it is clear there was something about this combination that brought out the best in Getz, especially at bright tempos. Take, for example, 'Smiles' and 'This Can't Be Love', both paced at around 60 bars a minute, not excessive but lively enough. They grip the attention quite mercilessly, not by swagger or bombast but by the sheer fluency and freshness of the improvised line. One cannot help noticing the immaculate technique, the precise articulation and the beauty of tone, but these are only the means by which an extraordinary mind expresses itself. Stan Levey put it well when he said, "The horn was an expression of his head. There were no barriers. The music just came rolling out."[5]

Eight pieces were recorded at the session, of which six went to make up an album entitled *Award Winner*, one appeared on *The Soft Swing* and one unaccountably remained unissued until complete editions began to appear in the 1990s. This was a version of 'But Beautiful', one of Jimmy Van Heusen's finest melodies and a great favourite with Getz. He had known it since the Herman days, when it was one of Woody's vocal features. Comparing this gorgeous 1957 version with his ballad recordings of a few years earlier illustrates very clearly the change that has taken place in his tone. Even the highest notes, which earlier would have had a fluting weightlessness to them, now sound lusty and full-throated.

Meanwhile, back in the real world, to Getz's financial woes had been added chaos in his family arrangements. After her divorce, Beverly had taken up with Tony Fruscella, of all people. She also had charge of the children, and all five of them were living together in extreme squalor. The police raided their apartment and arrested Fruscella for drug possession. Beverly fled, abandoning the children to the care of Stan's mother, and there was every likelihood they would be placed in a foster home. After all, their father was a convicted felon and bankrupt, their mother a hopeless drug addict, and their new stepmother little more than a girl herself, and a foreigner at that. Eventually the court gave custody to Stan's parents, Goldie and Al, and for all practical purposes the children passed into the care of Stan and Monica Getz.

Once more without a band of his own, Getz joined a JATP tour in September. Norman Granz set up recording sessions during gaps in the schedule, featuring the musicians in various combinations. The first of these studio sessions took place on October 10th, featuring Getz with the Oscar Peterson Trio. Nothing could be further in atmosphere from the Levy-Vinnegar sessions than this. The Peterson trio of the 1950s – completed by Herb Ellis on guitar and Ray Brown on bass – was the perfect swing machine, well-oiled and inexorable. The three of them had worked long and hard on it until the group was, in Ray Brown's oft-quoted phrase, "damn near waterproof".

It was not for nothing that Peterson's biographer, Gene Lees, entitled his book *The Will To Swing*. 'I Want To Be Happy', the first number on the album, although actually last in the order of recording, presents a formidable demonstration of Peterson's unstoppable drive and urgency. Peterson is not being competitive here, in the Sonny Stitt style, but neither is he providing discreet support, like Lou Levy. He is creating the kind of impetus that would keep any soloist airborne, and Getz revels in it. His playing communicates all the freedom and exhilaration of the experience. More than the usual number of Lester-isms make their appearance in this solo, testimony no doubt to the continuing influence of Lester's own celebrated version of the same tune, recorded with Peterson's hero, Nat Cole, back in 1945. The music from the Peterson session is not only blissfully uplifting, but infinitely varied too. Alongside the bravura 'I Want To Be Happy' come the simple, breezy 'Pennies From Heaven', the serene 'I'm Glad There Is You' and two poignant single-chorus ballads, 'Bewitched' and 'Polka Dots And Moonbeams', opening and closing the inevitable medley. At around this time Getz seems to have become keen on the idea of raising the key by a semitone towards the end of a piece. 'Pennies From Heaven' shifts from C to D-flat after the piano solo, and the last eight bars of 'Polka Dots' suddenly emerge resplendently attired in E major, like an unexpected ray of sunshine.

GETZ MEETS...

There is more recorded Getz dating from October 1957 than from any other month of his life. The Peterson session was followed the next day by a date under the leadership of Herb Ellis. It featured Getz, trumpeter Roy Eldridge, Ray Brown and Stan Levey. The album was released under the title *Nothing But The Blues*, and all eight numbers are either blues or blues-style pieces. Getz plays well enough, and sounds especially happy on the two Dixieland standards, 'Royal Garden Blues' and 'Tin Roof Blues', but the whole thing bears the unmistakable signs of a good idea that didn't quite come off. Everyone is trying a little too hard to fit into a formula, not helped by some fairly scrappy ensemble playing.

On the next day, October 12th, Getz was teamed with Gerry Mulligan and a rhythm section consisting of Lou Levy, Ray Brown and Stan Levey. It was clearly a relaxed and enjoyable session, although nothing momentous emerged. The most interesting parts of the resulting album, variously named *Getz Meets Mulligan, Mulligan Meets Getz, Getz Meets Mulligan In Hi-Fi*, and so on, are the two numbers in which they exchange instruments. They are still just about recognisable, but they surrender their distinctive tones and lose most of their individuality in the process.

A few days later Getz appeared on Nat King Cole's TV show. Cole was the first African-American singing star to have his own network television show. He had fought hard to get it, arguing that if Sinatra and Perry Como had TV shows, why shouldn't he? NBC eventually gave him the show, but it proved impossible to find enough sponsors to pay for it. *The Nat King Cole Show* ran for 15 months before NBC finally pulled the plug. One reason it lasted as long as it did was the willingness of Nat's friends to appear as guests on the show, often for nominal payment. Tony Bennett, Peggy Lee, Harry Belafonte, Eartha Kitt, The Hi-Los – it was probably the most impressive guest list ever. On October 15th 1957 the guests were Norman Granz and the entire JATP company. In his earlier career, as one of the finest jazz pianists of his generation, Nat himself had played with JATP, so the old pals' act came into the picture here, too.

The surviving telerecording, later transferred to videotape, is a valuable record of the mid-fifties JATP, and one of the few moving images of Stan Getz dating from this time. He plays 'I Want To Be Happy' in a quintet with Cole on piano, Eldridge, Ray Brown and Jo Jones, and joins Eldridge, Coleman Hawkins and the Peterson trio, plus Jo Jones, in 'Stompin' At The Savoy', with Cole singing a chorus. Age and repeated transfers from one medium to another have affected the sound quality, but Getz plays an excellent solo on the second number. He remains completely expressionless throughout and, interestingly, closes his eyes, instead of maintaining his customary blank stare. In repose, he looks just like any presentable, 30-year-old, white American professional man. If it were not for the saxophone in his hands you would guess that he worked in a bank, or possibly in the more sober side of advertising.

Granz had modified his original policy of cramming as many famous names as possible together on a stage and letting them fight it out. Instead, he now favoured a varied programme of smaller groups, usually a couple of soloists plus Peterson's trio and a drummer. One such pairing which proved particularly successful on the 1957 tour was that of Stan Getz and the trombonist JJ Johnson. As the partnership with Brookmeyer had amply demonstrated, tenor saxophone and trombone blend very well, although Johnson was stylistically Brookmeyer's opposite. His prodigious speed and agility was accompanied by a hard, bright tone and sharply defined articulation. His musical vocabulary was rooted in bebop but, like Getz, he had fashioned an individual approach which did not fall into any handy category.

Their portion of the programme was recorded twice during the tour, once at Chicago's Civic Opera House and again at the Shrine Auditorium in Los Angeles. This fact has caused endless bafflement to discographers and annotators over the years, because of the chaotic manner in which Granz chose to compile and release the subsequent albums. Even one of the dates is uncertain. What we undoubtedly have is two shows, almost identical in repertoire, one recorded in early stereo and the other in mono. The mono set is marginally better than the stereo one, partly because, in the latter, the rhythm section drags noticeably during the opening number, Charlie Parker's 'Billie's Bounce'. Generally speaking, however, there is little to choose between them, and the level of inspiration remains high throughout. Both versions of 'Crazy Rhythm' become almost unbearably exciting during Getz's solos and the subsequent passages of duet improvisation. The mono version of Getz's solo feature, 'It Never Entered My Mind', stands among his finest ballad performances. Set in the unlikely key of B major, it shadows Richard Rodgers's melody quite closely throughout, with sparse decoration and the most subtle of alterations. There is more air in the sound here than ever before. The climax comes with a sudden and devastating key change to G major for the final eight bars of the song, followed by a lovely melodic coda.

As soon as the tour was over, Getz took part in a session with Ella Fitzgerald and an orchestra conducted by Frank DeVol, for her album *Like Someone In Love*. His tenor simply provides brief obbligato passages around the vocal line on four songs – 'There's A Lull In My Life', 'You're Blasé', 'What Will I Tell My Heart?' and 'Midnight Sun' – but they are so eloquent and well-judged that they add immeasurably to the final result.

Getz's career was beginning to fall into a pattern that applied to the majority of JATP regulars, namely a string of epic JATP tours punctuated by such other work as could be fitted in around them. For the remainder of 1957 and into the following year he toured as a solo act. In February 1958 he recorded a pleasant album with the vibraphonist Cal Tjader in San Francisco. Its most significant feature, in retrospect, is that it marked the recording debut of two exceptional young musicians, bassist Scott LaFaro and drummer Billy Higgins, both of whom were to become major names in jazz. In the same month came a further encounter with Chet Baker, this time in a Chicago recording studio. The atmosphere seems to have been distinctly frosty. Certainly, neither of them performs with much distinction on the album *Stan Meets Chet*, although Getz's solo version of 'What's New?' has all his customary elegance and aplomb. The less said about the rhythm section the better.

Monica was pregnant. She was determined that the child should be born in Sweden, where she would have her family around her and be able to benefit from the famously efficient, and free, Swedish health service. For Getz himself, the future must have looked very much like the recent past – JATP tours, temporary bands, record sessions, airports, together with the constant attentions of drug peddlers, police and the IRS. The monotony might occasionally be broken by the reappearance of Beverly, *in extremis* yet again, or by another episode of uncontrollable behaviour on his own part. It was not an inviting prospect. He was due to join JATP for a European tour in April. He would drop off after the final concert, join Monica in Sweden and take stock of the future.

The Young Stan

Stan Getz (centre) outside the stage door at New York's Apollo Theater in 1950 (1). Playing alto saxophone (extreme right) with Jack Teagarden, 1943 (2). Early EP compilation of 1949 tracks for Sittin' In With label (3). Swedish Metronome 78rpm release of 'The Lady In Red' (4). First British release from Getz's 1951 Swedish visit, 'Standinavian' was Getz's new, punning title for 'Dear Old Stockholm' (5). French CD compilation of very early recordings with Teagarden, Kenton, Goodman etc (6).

Stan Getz NOBODY ELSE BUT ME

The Award Winner

84

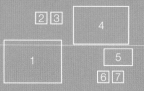

2 3

4

1

5

6 7

Classic Woody Herman saxophone section, Getz at extreme left (1). Getz's first live album (2). Original cover of *West Coast Jazz*, the album containing the stupendous 'Shine' solo (3). Recording session for *The Benny Goodman Story*, with Buck Clayton (trumpet) and Urbie Green (trombone) (4). Getz's first quintet, with guitarist Jimmy Raney, at Boston's Storyville Club (5). *The Steamer*, from 1956, includes the beautiful ballad 'You're Blasé' and stomping 'Blues For Mary Jane' (6). This picture (7) was first used to accompany Getz's 'thank you' advert to readers of *Down Beat* for voting him number one in their poll. The child is his son Steve.

Scandinavian Years

Escape to the simple life; Denmark 1958 (1). Getz lands in Stockholm (2). Jan Johansson, Oscar Pettiford, Getz and drummer Joe Harris in Copenhagen, 1959 (3). At the Blue Note in Paris, Getz indicates Lester Young's famous pork-pie hat, hanging above (4). Compilation of Getz recordings with European big bands (5). JJ Johnson, Getz's partner on the famous *Opera House* album (6). *Down Beat* cover announcing Getz's move to Europe (7). Getz with Jan Johansson, one of his favourite accompanists (8). Getz and guitarist Jimmy Gourley and drummer Kenny Clarke in Paris, 1960 (9).

Stan Getz   NOBODY ELSE BUT ME

In Focus

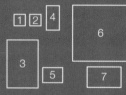

The classic *Focus* album (1). Getz and Brookmeyer reunited, 1961 (2). Getz in action shortly after returning home (3). Newly arrived in the US (4). Roy Haynes (5) featured in 'I'm Late, I'm Late', on the *Focus* album. Getz in Boston, 1962, with bassist John Neves and pianist Ray Santisi (6). Getz meets his old boss, Benny Goodman (7).

Play the Bossa Nova

Roy Haynes, Chuck Israels, Gary Burton and Getz at the Philharmonie, Berlin, 1966 (1). João Gilberto, Antonio Carlos Jobim and Stan Getz at the height of bossa nova (2). The words 'bossa nova' appeared nowhere on Getz's first Brazilian-style album (3). The finest bossa nova album of all, *Getz/Gilberto* (4). Guitarist Charlie Byrd (5) introduced Getz to the new music from Brazil and collaborated with him on *Jazz Samba*. Getz and Astrud Gilberto in Berlin, 1966 (6).

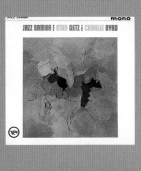

Stan Getz NOBODY ELSE BUT ME

Sweet Rain

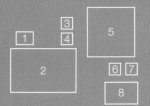

Guitarist Jim Hall (1) collaborated with Getz on *A Song After Sundown*. In 1970 Getz formed a quartet with British musicians (2) for a European tour: Spike Wells (drums), Ron Matthewson (bass), Mick Pyne (piano). Original *Sweet Rain* album cover, 1967 (3). The only studio album by the Getz-Burton quartet, 1964 (4). Getz and Chet Baker at Newport, 1964 (5). Original *Dynasty* double album (6). *A Song After Sundown*, recorded at Tanglewood, includes Getz's final collaboration with Eddie Sauter (7). Pensive in Copenhagen, 1968 (8).

Stay Current

Despite bouts of illness, Getz continued to play at his best in the late 1980s (1, 6). Keeping up-to-date in 1972: original LP *Captain Marvel* (2). Towards the end of Getz's electric, rock influenced period came an album featuring guitarist Chuck Loeb (3). Getz returned to a purely acoustic quartet in the early 1980s, with albums like *The Dolphin* (4). Getz is greeted by guitarist Emily Remler (right) at the Nice Jazz Festival, 1987 (5). Tony Williams (7), drummer on *Captain Marvel*. Getz with Gerry Mulligan in 1980 (8).

Pure Getz

1	
2	4
3	

Victor Lewis, long-serving member of Getz's later quartets (1). Superb 1982 album *Pure Getz* (2). Getz shows the strain at Nice Jazz Festival, 1987 (3). Performing in London in 1990, less than a year before his death (4).

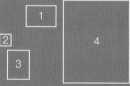

CHAPTER 9

Fine
And Dandy

"I'm tired of competition. I'm tired of tearing around making money ... I wanted to find peace of mind."

GETZ EXPLAINS HIS RELOCATION TO DENMARK

AT THE END OF THE 1950s

The JATP company that left for Europe in April 1958 was a large one. It included Eldridge, Gillespie, Getz, Stitt, Hawkins, the Oscar Peterson trio, pianist Lou Levy, bassist Max Bennett, drummers Jo Jones and Gus Johnson, plus Ella Fitzgerald. Norman Granz's strategy was to present the entire show at a few large events, such as the Brussels World's Fair, and at other times divide them into various smaller combinations that could appear separately. It was as a result of this arrangement that a package of two bands, headed by Getz and Hawkins respectively, briefly toured Britain in May.

On the 17th, an enterprising sound engineer recorded the proceedings at the Free Trade Hall, Manchester. Since this seems to have been achieved by means of a feed from the PA system, the saxophone sounds a little distant, but Getz plays with the relaxed fluency that the presence of Lou Levy always brought out in him. He plays several old favourites, such as 'That Old Feeling' and 'All God's Children Got Rhythm', but the best is his only recorded performance of the venerable Basie riff tune 'Taps Miller', complete with two

Coleman Hawkins checks out Stan's technique, while Ella sings

stop-time choruses. There's also a further version of 'It Never Entered My Mind', following exactly the pattern of the Chicago Opera House recording – key change, coda and all.

Getz did not go straight to Sweden after the final concert of the JATP tour, because he had picked up a string of gigs in France. This was increasingly becoming a pattern. American musicians would travel to Europe as part of a package show and stay on for a while to play clubs or festivals. He was in Paris for the second half of June, where a concert at the Olympia Music Hall was broadcast. For this he was accompanied by Martial Solal on piano, Pierre Michelot on bass and the pioneering bebop drummer Kenny Clarke, who had become a prominent fixture of the Paris jazz scene. Clarke's robust playing certainly lights a spark under the numbers that survive from this session. In fact, 'All God's Children...' comes over almost as a tenor-and-drums duet with piano and bass accompaniment, an impression which is not entirely due to the recording balance. After a stop-time chorus, halfway through Getz's solo, the famously demonstrative French audience erupts in a storm of cheering and applause.

There is also a glowing version of the ballad 'Ghost Of A Chance', forever associated with Lester Young because of his sombre but magnificent 1944 recording. At one point Clarke makes it plain that he wants to double the tempo, an invitation which Getz studiously ignores. To double the tempo on a ballad, rather than hint delicately at the possibility without actually doing it, is almost always a mistake, and a vulgar one at that.

On July 13th he appeared at the *Festival du Jazz* at Cannes, in a line-up of five tenor saxophonists – three Americans (himself, Coleman Hawkins and Don Byas), one Frenchman (Guy Lafitte) and one Franco-American (Barney Wilen). The broadcast result is interesting rather than edifying. He then repaired to Sweden, to the von Rosen lakeside estate of Rockelstad, to make the acquaintance of his new-born daughter, Pamela. It was only then that he finally made up his mind about settling in Scandinavia.

Looked at from a conventional point of view, this might seem a disastrous career move for a world-famous jazz musician, aged only 31 and still topping the polls. But, as we have seen, there was the question of getting away from the drug culture, and the accumulated shambles of his life in the US. There was also the powerful attraction exerted by Europe on American jazz musicians at that period. America was the home of jazz music, but Europe liked to think of itself as the home of jazz appreciation. It is no accident that the first jazz discography was compiled by a Frenchman, Charles Delaunay.

European jazz lovers had learned about jazz through recordings, and tended to regard records as authentic and definitive texts. If a musician had played on even a single prestigious recording date, his name would be known to aficionados. If he were someone of the stature of, say, Dexter Gordon, he would be honoured and lionised. "Back home I was just a saxophone player," Gordon once remarked, "but here I'm a saxophonist."[1] Gordon came to Europe in 1962, to play a two-week engagement at Ronnie Scott's club in London, and did not return home for 14 years. Similar stories are attached to dozens of names – Kenny Clarke, Ben Webster, Art Farmer, Bud Powell, the list goes on and on. For Getz, there was the added attraction that this was his wife's homeland, that her family was a prominent one and thus able to smooth the path in many small, practical ways.

It was decided that they would settle in Denmark, in the Copenhagen suburb of Lyngby, a short ferry journey across the Oresund, the stretch of water that separates Denmark from Sweden. Copenhagen is the largest and most cosmopolitan of Scandinavian cities, with good connections to the rest of Europe. It boasted the country's leading jazz club, the Montmartre, and the studios of the national broadcasting corporation, Danmarks Radio, both of which were to figure prominently in Getz's professional life there. He also formed a close friendship with bassist Oscar Pettiford, who was already well established in Copenhagen.

GETZ AT LARGE

Early in 1960, during Getz's Scandinavian sojourn, *Down Beat* magazine ran a major feature on him, headed 'The Expatriate Life of Stan Getz.' It describes very well the routine of his new life and the attraction it held for him. "The Getz family has sunk itself into the life of Denmark," wrote the reporter. "His children, with the linguistic ease of the young, have come to speak fluent Danish, and one of them even appeared recently in a play at his school ... Getz himself speaks only a few words of Danish. 'It's impossible to learn,' he says. 'Besides, everybody in Denmark speaks English and everybody wants to practise his English on you.'" (On the other hand, Dexter Gordon appeared to have little difficulty with the language, judging from a television interview clip in which the Danish interviewer asks him a question in English and Gordon answers in Danish.)

"All the evidence suggests that Stan Getz has found in his expatriate life more health and happiness than his career has ever before given him... 'I'm tired of competition. I'm tired of tearing around making money,' says Getz who, until he settled in Denmark, was constantly on the go with concert tours, the nightclub circuit and recording work, among many activities. 'There are other things in life than making money. Here I have more time for my family. I don't make as much money as in the States, but it's cheaper to live here. And it's unhurried. I enjoy the relaxed way of living in Europe. I wanted to find peace of mind. That's hard to find in the States.'"

The article goes on to list a number of prominent jazz musicians who had recently settled in Europe ("fugitives from personal problems... the Age of Anxiety... racial discrimination... the disjointed family life that is so often forced on the American jazzman") and to note the growing friendship between Getz and Pettiford, before passing on to describe the Copenhagen jazz scene, in particular the Montmartre.

"The Montmartre has no sign outside its door. Indeed, it has no other identifying mark than a giant photo of Count Basie that stares at you from the outside wall. Yet jazz fans and musicians have no trouble finding it. They gravitate towards it with the unerring instinct of a Sahara desert camel galloping towards an oasis for replenishment ...The Montmartre is dark and smoky, lit only by candles that cast long, moving shadows, like claws, across the walls."

The writer goes on to explain that the clientele ("hipsters") sit on benches "at rough-hewn tables, sipping heady Danish beer". The girls look like Brigitte Bardot, and the men wear beards and smoke pipes. "They look terribly earnest and sit in frozen postures while the musicians are blowing ... the boor who dares to tap a finger to the rhythm is caught in a crossfire of a dozen icy stares."

Stan Getz NOBODY ELSE BUT ME

Turning to the subject of local musicians, *Down Beat* picks out two in particular, the pianist Jan Johansson and drummer William Schiopffe, both of whom played and recorded with Getz during this period. European jazz at the time was still very much the apprentice of American jazz, as Johansson frankly admitted: "American musicians like Stan and Oscar not only play better than most Europeans, but in many ways quite different from us. They have more nuances, they are more forceful, bolder. The rest of us are so busy trying to keep up with them that we rarely reach the great moments."[2] A few years later, when European musicians did start to become bolder and more forceful, some Americans, Getz included, were not always best pleased.

A fair amount of recorded material survives from Getz's two-and-a-half-year stay in Europe. His contract with Granz was still in force and he made several albums for Granz's Verve label, often with a mixture of local musicians and expatriate Americans. In August 1958, soon after his arrival, there was a session at Sweden's Europa film studios, with the Swedish producer Simon Brehm acting as Granz's proxy. Taking part were Johansson and Schiopffe, bassist Gunnar Johnson, Erik Nordstrom in the unenviable position of second tenor saxophone, and two of Sweden's star soloists, trombonist Ake Persson and baritone saxophonist Lars Gullin. The band was completed by the trumpeter Benny Bailey, who had jumped ship at the end of a Lionel Hampton tour in 1953 and thereafter spent most of his career in Scandinavia. Schiopffe is perhaps a little over-eager, but in other respects the band sounds remarkably relaxed. It's noticeable, though, that Getz plays more simply than usual, as if reluctant to take chances. The album, *Imported From Europe*, took three sessions to complete.

It was more usual for Getz either to perform with a quartet or to appear as a guest star with an existing band. Notable among these was the Ib Glindemann Orchestra, a big-band roughly patterned after Kenton's. Glindemann himself was aged only 24 at the time of his collaboration with Getz. His main instrument was the trumpet, but his role in the band was that of arranger and conductor. On live recordings from their concerts together, Getz sounds completely at home, even in a version of 'Cherokee' at around 70 bars a minute, where he comes bubbling cheerfully out over the ensemble in fine style. 'Don't Get Around Much Anymore' and 'My Funny Valentine' are two more particularly successful numbers. Glindemann later went on to a career in conducting, in both the symphonic and popular music worlds.

YOU'RE MY SINGER

As time went on, Getz's European accompanists began to relax into their role. As remarks already quoted have shown, he was an effective and businesslike bandleader and, in normal circumstances, a sympathetic one. In one of his moods, however, he could be cutting and deeply unpleasant. He once rounded on a young bassist who had the temerity to check his tuning while he, Getz, was announcing the next number. "You practise in your pad. You come here to work. Do that once more and you're fired," he snapped. He fired him at the end of the night anyway.[3]

Fortunately Johansson, Schiopffe and bassist Daniel Jordan, who often constituted his 'home' rhythm section, seem to have been in favour most of the time. Their playing on the Verve album *Stan Getz At Large*, recorded in Copenhagen in January 1960, is firm and confident throughout. The set includes a particularly effective version of 'The Folks Who Live On The Hill', complete with its rarely heard introductory verse.

From his home base in Denmark, Getz was able to travel easily throughout continental Europe, especially to France and Germany, and there are live recordings and fragments of broadcasts from as far afield as Warsaw. In the spring of 1959 he played for several weeks at the Blue Note in Paris, following Lester Young. Calling in at the club a few days before he was due to begin his engagement, he encountered Lester propping up the bar. Fixing Getz with a long gaze, Lester said, "Lady Getz, you're my singer." Recalling, no doubt, the exchange with Sonny Stitt a few years earlier ("Now sing me a song..."), Getz took this as a compliment on a par with his hero's very first words to him, back in 1945 – "Nice eyes, Pres. Carry on." This was their last meeting. Pres died on March 15th, soon after arriving back in New York.

At the Blue Note in Paris, Getz was accompanied by the Franco-American house band, normally consisting of Rene Urtreger (piano), Jimmy Gourley (guitar), Jean-Marie Ingrand (bass) and Kenny Clarke (drums) – a splendid ensemble in its own right. The few recorded examples of Getz with this band are so sharp and full of energy that the absence of a proper studio session is a cause of real regret. One number in particular, Tadd Dameron's 'Lady Bird', arouses memories of the great 1951 Storyville session, partly because the instrumentation is the same, but also because they all sound so relaxed in each other's company.

Clarke was always a powerful and active drummer, but his playing was unfailingly apposite. He drove the band along without ever distracting the soloist or causing collisions in the rhythm section. Urtreger had, by this time, played piano for virtually every major soloist visiting the French capital. He was therefore more experienced than many of his US peers and, rather like Al Haig, he was able to sum up a soloist's needs in an instant. Gourley, born in St Louis in 1926, was, like Kenny Clarke, permanently resident in Paris. In his early career he had followed Jimmy Raney through several bands, and their styles were broadly similar. He was largely responsible for introducing the cool, single-line electric guitar sound to a French jazz scene still deeply under the influence of Django Reinhardt's fiery, gipsy approach. Ingrand was one of the two French bassists that visiting Americans inevitably asked for, the other being Pierre Michelot.

These four come together beautifully with Getz on 'Lady Bird'. The simple head arrangement, with Gourley providing a complementary line to Getz, and the rhythm section emphasising the accents in the melody, gives shape and a purposeful air to the performance. Getz clearly feels no constraint as he swings through four choruses, the first two backed only by bass and drums. It is not, perhaps, one of his greatest solos, but it has a wonderfully carefree spirit. It's not entirely clear where 'Lady Bird' and its companion pieces, 'Dear Old Stockholm' and 'Cherokee' were recorded. It may have been in the Blue Note itself, although the lack of ambient nightclub noise and the volume of the applause suggest a concert. Whatever the case, the recording balance is exceptionally good.

Stan Getz

In May 1994, almost three years after his death, a charming tale concerning Getz in Paris appeared in the British daily newspaper *The Independent*. It was told by a property developer and jazz fan named Chris Marshall about an adventure he had undertaken as a schoolboy in the late 1950s. These are the bones of his story: "I read in the *Melody Maker* that Stan Getz was coming to Paris. I was very excited as he was my hero, and I had the strongest urge to go and hear him play." Having told his mother he would be staying with a school friend over the weekend, he left school early on Friday and hitch-hiked, via Dover and Calais, to Paris. There he found a cheap hotel and located the Blue Note. The following evening he turned up at the club, far too early, ordered a beer and sat at a front table. Eventually more people turned up. "They seemed arty and exotic. This was a great deal more stylish than the Croydon Jazz Club."

At around midnight Getz came on. "He introduced each number, and spoke in French and English. The music was fabulous. I was completely mesmerised. I couldn't believe I was listening to him. I must have been really conspicuous sitting at the front on my own ... After his set, Stan Getz himself came over to my table. 'Say, sonny,' he said, 'where have you come from?... England! My God!' And he sat down and started talking to me. I explained how I'd read he was going to be in Paris, and that I'd hitch-hiked to see him. He thought that was very funny. 'Hey, man, you must be my number-one fan,' he laughed. 'Would you like another beer?'... When the beer arrived he asked, 'Are you hungry?' I said I was, so he ordered me an enormous steak sandwich ... and we continued chatting for ages." Afterwards, "I couldn't believe what I'd experienced. I was quite awestruck. I wanted to talk to somebody about it but there was no-one around."

On his return home, young Marshall found that his subterfuge had been discovered, but his parents were so relieved to have him back safely that he escaped punishment. He still had the Blue Note menu card, signed: 'To Chris – Stan Getz.'

Apart from illustrating the fanatical enthusiasm for jazz among many young Britons, before the universal blizzard of pop culture engulfed the world, this story also reveals a kindly, unaffected, avuncular Getz – a picture totally at odds with the one drawn by others. A nice bunch of guys, indeed.

COOL VELVET

Lester Young may habitually have expressed himself in his own private language, but he had rare insight and often put his finger on important points that more loquacious and opinionated people missed. He heard in the lyrical, romantic side of Stan Getz the qualities he admired in his favourite singers, such as Billie Holiday, Frank Sinatra, Jo Stafford and Dick Haymes. He put it in those three words: "You're my singer" – and he was right.

It does seem strange, given the beauty of his tone and the overwhelmingly melodic character of his playing, that no-one had yet thought to record Stan Getz's tenor saxophone as a romantic voice, in an orchestral setting. The practice was by no means unknown in jazz. Gillespie and Parker had both recorded successfully with strings, as had Ben Webster, Clifford Brown, Bobby Hackett and numerous others. But it was not until March 1960, with an album entitled *Cool Velvet*, that Getz made his debut in this genre. It was arranged and conducted by Russell Garcia and recorded in Baden-Baden with a large string orchestra, plus vibraphone, harp (played by the deliciously named Blanche Birdsong) and a rhythm section with Jan Johansson on piano.

Jazz critics often display signs of acute discomfort when faced with records like *Cool Velvet*, dismissing them with the vaguely insulting term 'easy listening'. Easy listening, in this context, appears to mean something like 'music that is bland, insipid, undemanding and generally beneath the notice of discriminating tastes, such as our own'. It implies that jazz musicians are somehow letting the side down when they resort to such tactics, and prompted only by the basest commercial motives. The fact that the music is often engaging and delightful, sometimes even rising to heights of great beauty and passion, appears not to register. *Cool Velvet* falls squarely into the 'engaging and delightful' category – a set of ten songs, sympathetically arranged and performed by Getz with restrained elegance. His vast range of expression, from a subdued whisper to an exultant shout, really flowers in these surroundings.

One of the pieces is a gorgeous reworking of 'Early Autumn', approached not as the instrumental feature it originally was, but as the yearningly evocative song that Ralph Burns and Johnny Mercer subsequently made out of it. Other outstanding tracks include Benny Golson's 'Whisper Not', Mel Torme's 'I Was Born To Be Blue' and, yet again, 'It Never Entered My Mind' (still in B major, but this time without the key-change). Happily, there was more to come from Getz in this mode.

Oscar Pettiford died suddenly, of viral meningitis, on September 8th 1960. He was 37 and left a wife and two young children. On October 1st, Getz played at a memorial concert in Frederickberg, held for the benefit of Pettiford's family. The three recorded numbers that survive consist of two slow ballads, 'Spring Can Really Hang You Up The Most' and 'Without A Song', and his minor-key transposition of 'Get Happy'. The first of these is a touching piece of gentle melancholy, full of restrained pathos. The pianist is Bengt Hallberg, and no one could have provided a more apt and sympathetic accompaniment.

It's impossible to tell what part Pettiford's death played in turning Getz's thoughts towards returning to the US, but their friendship had been an important feature of his expatriate life and he must have felt the loss keenly. There were other factors, too. In 1960, for the first time in a decade, his name did not appear as top tenor saxophonist in the *Down Beat* readers' poll. Was this just a question of out of sight, out of mind, or was he genuinely becoming a back-number? Admittedly, all the other magazines (with the exception of France's *Jazz Hot*) still rated him Number One, but to someone as insecure as Getz the *Down Beat* result would have been a serious matter.

The name to replace his was that of John Coltrane, which made it doubly serious. Coltrane could not be written off as a passing fad. He represented a totally different approach to the instrument, as different from himself as Lester Young had been from Coleman Hawkins in the late 1930s. Getz had heard Coltrane in person and at length when the Miles Davis Quintet had toured Europe in March 1960. Indeed Getz, with Johansson, Ray Brown and Ed Thigpen, had shared the bill for most of that tour, which was a JATP production. Coltrane's playing had caused dismay among European audiences (he had even been booed by crowds in Germany) and outrage when he had refused to take part, along with Getz, in a televised jam session. But Getz recognised these reactions as the shock caused by something new, unfamiliar and very powerful. Coltrane presented not so much a threat as a challenge.

It has already been noted that, in some ways, Stan Getz resembled Benny Goodman. One of these was his need to be challenged. In the context of his reaction to Coltrane, it's instructive to read Gunther Schuller's description of Goodman's character: "It is in Goodman's nature and temperament that he easily gets bored with people, pieces, styles, and even his own playing. Part of this results, ironically, from the extraordinary levels of perfection he demands of himself ... and the apparent ease with which he himself maintains those high standards. That kind of ease and facility can become boring, because there are very few challenges which cannot instantly be met."[4]

This applies exactly to Getz, too. He had been getting bored, and now came the challenge which could not instantly be met. One thing was certain: he could not even begin to address the problem from his Scandinavian retreat. He would have to return to the United States.

CHAPTER 10

Focus

> *"I always left, at the back of my mind, a*
> *space for another part to be added ... The*
> *way he reacted to the environment of the*
> *orchestra was one of the most gratifying*
> *things I've ever experienced."*

EDDIE SAUTER, ON CO-CREATING THE

STAN GETZ MASTERWORK *FOCUS*

The final months of Getz's Scandinavian exile were largely taken up with a long JATP European tour, in which he was reunited with JJ Johnson and Dizzy Gillespie. The live recordings, from the Stockholm concert of November 21st, contain some vintage Getz-Johnson interplay, particularly in a high-spirited version of 'Sweet Georgia Brown', which amply confirms Getz's fondness for the open harmonies and broad melodies of Dixieland jazz.

This is not to say he actually plays in a Dixieland style, with Dixieland notes and phrasing, but whenever he gets into one of those old tunes his whole manner becomes easy and playful. He and Johnson even use the Dixieland format for the opening and closing themes of 'Sweet Georgia Brown', one playing the melody while the other capers and tumbles around it, then swapping roles. It was unusual, in those days, for 'modern' jazz musicians to do things like that, because there was still a certain enmity, dating back to the 1940s, between modernists and Dixieland traditionalists, whom the former called 'mouldy figs'. Getz, needless to say, never indulged in ideological tomfoolery of this kind.

Stan Getz in 1962, at the Monterey Jazz Festival

He may have been unsettled by his exposure to Coltrane, but there is no hint of confusion or uncertainty anywhere in this performance. By contrast, many established players were completely derailed by the Coltrane experience. Some, like Art Pepper, recovered later, whereas others, such as Harold Land, never quite did. If there had been some unconscious influence on Getz it would most likely have shown up in his feature number, Jerome Kern's 'Yesterdays', but this is absolutely pure Getz throughout. In fact, 'Yesterdays' is startlingly good, even by his standards. He infuses the piece with a strong element of blues, and plays the not-quite-doubling-tempo game with a masterly touch. The rhythm section of Victor Feldman, Sam Jones and Louis Hayes play it perfectly too.

The Getz family returned to the United States, with many misgivings on Monica's part, in January 1961. Before following them there, it might be as well to consider what had been happening in jazz while they had been away, and how much of it Getz himself might have heard. Broadly speaking, there were four movements or strands of development: modal jazz, soul jazz, hard bop and free jazz. They interwove to a certain extent, but each had its identifying characteristics. The one which can be described in purely musical terms, and which had the most far-reaching effect, is modal jazz. The history of jazz up until the late 1950s can fairly be described as one of continuous harmonic sophistication. Bebop, as described in Chapter Three, was a particularly large step, but still only a stage in a progress which led, over the course of 60 years, from the harmonic vocabulary of simple military marches and three-chord blues to the edge of the chromatic universe of Debussy and Ravel.

As the harmonies grew denser, improvising on them came to resemble an obstacle course, more a matter of ingenuity than melodic invention. It was Miles Davis who found a way out of this impasse, first in 1958, with a piece entitled 'Milestones', but most significantly with his album *Kind Of Blue* recorded in the spring of 1959. Instead of being based on a sequence of chords linked together in a chain and moving briskly through a series of temporary key changes, the *Kind Of Blue* music is built on static harmonies – one chord for four or eight bars, followed by another. Each chord implies a set of notes, and these are the ones the improviser uses. The term 'modal' became attached to this system because the set of notes formed a scale, and the commonly used term for non-standard scales is 'modes'. John Coltrane was a member of the band that made *Kind Of Blue*, and for much of his subsequent career he worked with modal structures.

It was almost exactly a year later that the Miles Davis Quintet toured Europe, sharing the bill with a Getz quartet. Judging by the surviving broadcast recordings, they played substantially the same set each night and it included two numbers off *Kind Of Blue* – 'All Blues' and 'So What' – so Getz would have become very familiar with them. He may, of course, have owned the *Kind Of Blue* album, although he does not seem to have listened to records very much in his mature life.

Soul jazz was the name given to a back-to-the-roots movement among African-American musicians. This, too, sought simplicity, but sought it in the forms and practices of blues and gospel music. Cannonball Adderley and Getz's former pianist Horace Silver were among its leading lights and scored great success with catchy numbers such as 'Sack O' Woe' and 'Sermonette' (Adderley) and 'The Preacher' and 'Sister

Sadie' (Silver). Soul jazz was, as much as anything, an expression of black solidarity and black pride at a time of growing racial ferment in the United States. By its very nature, soul jazz would have had no direct musical influence on Stan Getz, although he was to find that it had the effect of disparaging all white musicians by implying that they could not be authentic.

Hard bop was the converse of cool, and associated with New York and the eastern seaboard in the same way as cool was identified with Los Angeles and the west coast. As its name suggests, hard bop was the energetic and dynamic descendant of bebop. Its outlines tended to be simpler and a buoyant assertiveness replaced the edgy neurosis which had never been far below the surface of early bebop. The great figures of hard bop included Max Roach, Clifford Brown (until his early death in 1956), Sonny Rollins, Art Blakey's Jazz Messengers (in their many incarnations) and, confusingly, the Horace Silver Quintet. Indeed, the dividing lines between hard bop, soul jazz and modal jazz were often more theoretical than actual. The leading jazz record labels of the time, Blue Note, Riverside and Prestige, tended to treat them all as parts of the same phenomenon.

JAZZ THERAPY

Free jazz took many shapes, but the one most immediately likely to affect Getz was that played by Ornette Coleman. His music was free in the sense that it did away with the concept of regular form and conventional harmony, although it mostly retained the straightforward, swinging beat of jazz. Coleman himself composed some tremendously catchy themes, such as 'Lonely Woman', 'Tears Inside' and 'When Will The Blues Leave?', that at first led listeners to expect 'normal' solos to follow them, which didn't happen. Coleman and his trumpet partner, Don Cherry, created their solos purely by following a melodic and rhythmic idea wherever it might take them. Although it didn't apply to Coleman, there was a fearful amount of anger in many free players, so much so that their music often sounded more like therapy for the player than entertainment for the listener. Free jazz came complete with an army of spokesmen, proselytisers and ideologues, most of whom used the word 'free' to conflate the notions of artistic and political freedom. Since there was no way of telling if a free musician was any good or not, the whole movement degenerated into an adventure playground for pseuds and chancers. There is an apocryphal story about Stan Getz and Coleman Hawkins sitting stony-faced in a dark corner of a jazz club while a celebrated free saxophonist did his stuff. At last Hawkins turned to Getz and murmured, "Stanley, he's playing our song."

These new forms and styles had not suddenly sprung into existence during Getz's absence. Hard bop, for instance, had been brewing since the early 1950s. But when they all burst vigorously forth towards the end of the decade the entire jazz climate changed dramatically. The phenomenon was part of the general shift in sensibility that marked those few years, a time when the post-war certainties were beginning to falter. Affluence might not go on increasing forever. The social order might not remain stable. The next generation might not want the world that their parents had wanted, and had striven so industriously to create. So, when Getz arrived back in New York aboard the Swedish liner Kungsholm, on January 19th 1961, he found himself in an environment that looked the same but felt disconcertingly different.

"It was common knowledge in the music world that the return of Stan Getz was not accorded the treatment usually expected for a conquering hero returned from overseas battle,"[1] wrote Leonard Feather, looking back on the event. Indeed, to begin with, Getz had difficulty finding any suitable work at all. "The cool sound and the cool attitude had given way, during those two or three years, to a concern for heavy, aggressive statement, to an atmosphere of racial hostility without precedent in jazz, to an accent on musical anger and disregard for fundamentals – characteristics that were not be found in the light lyricism of a Stan Getz solo."[2]

As soon as he could, Getz had put together a quartet, consisting of himself, one of his favourite drummers, Roy Haynes, and two brilliant young players, pianist Steve Kuhn and bassist Scott LaFaro. This was the band with which he made his New York return debut, on March 23rd, at the Village Vanguard. The reviews were enthusiastic, but the atmosphere was, by all accounts, pretty poisonous. Bill Coss, who reviewed the event for *Down Beat*, was certainly aware of it. "There were in attendance the haters, musical and otherwise," Coss wrote, "who came to find out whether the young white man, who had long ago lengthened the legendary and unorthodox Lester Young line into something of his own, could stand up against what is, in current jazz, at least a revolution from it (or revulsion about it)."[3]

From the few recorded examples available, the band sounds excellent. Haynes could not make all Getz's engagements, in which case his replacement was Pete La Rocca. The bulk of the album they recorded for Verve remains unissued, but there is one outstanding track, a blistering version of Sonny Rollins's 'Airegin'. In its way, this is as impressive as 'Shine' – it is as fluent and imaginative, but more angular and abstract, and does not have that 'falling off a log' sense of ease. But then, of course, it would be difficult to find two tunes more different in character that 'Shine' and 'Airegin'. ('Airegin', incidentally, is simply 'Nigeria' spelt backwards.) One thing that does come across strongly is LaFaro's brilliance. For his first two solo choruses, Getz is accompanied by bass and drums only, and you can practically hear the delight Getz and LaFaro must have taken in the way tenor and bass swing along together. Getz had probably not experienced bass playing as sharp as this since the death of his friend Oscar Pettiford. But the partnership was shortlived. LaFaro died in a car crash in July of that year.

FILLING A HOLE

Getz's difficulties did not ease when he took the band to the west coast. In Hollywood, they followed the Miles Davis Quintet into a club and business was so bad that the proprietor cancelled the week-night performances and they played only at weekends. In San Francisco, where Coltrane was appearing simultaneously at a rival club, Getz drew very meagre houses. Looking back on this time a few years later, Monica Getz recalled: "Many true jazz aficionados had quit coming, being confused and bored. Only old friends like Miles and Diz gave him solace and hope and worried with him about the direction of jazz. It was heart-breaking to see his old defences coming back."[4] On top of everything else, Norman Granz had just sold the Verve label and the new owners, MGM, were getting itchy for some saleable product, possibly something along the lines of *Cool Velvet*. But Getz refused all their suggestions, because he had an ambitious recording project of his own in mind. The roots of it went back a long way – back, in fact, to 1945, when he had played in Benny Goodman's band.

The big-band era produced all kinds of delayed-action results. Virtually all the great vocalists of the 1950s began their careers as band singers, and the experience gave them attributes that no later generation ever quite matched, such as rhythmic poise, clear diction and all-round musicianship. At the same time, the Hollywood studios were filled with instrumentalists who had gravitated there after years on the road with bandleaders like Goodman, Dorsey and Harry James. Just as important, although less conspicuous, were the arrangers. They created the sounds that became the background music of the western world, on film soundtracks, radio, records, and eventually television: Paul Weston and Axel Stordahl, ex-Tommy Dorsey arrangers; Billy May, ex-Glenn Miller; Nelson Riddle, ex-Charlie Spivak; Henry Mancini, ex-Tex Beneke, and many more. Towards the end of the big-band era, as the bands grew bigger and more expert, some arrangers became more and more adventurous, pushing the boundaries of conventional dance music.

When Getz was with Goodman he had been very taken with the arrangements of Eddie Sauter, composer of Goodman showpieces, such as 'Clarinet à la King' and 'Benny Rides Again'. Sauter, a Juilliard graduate, commanded a huge reputation among musicians. When most big-band writers were sticking to the reliable formula of segregating the brass and saxophone sections and employing them to create blocks of sound, Sauter followed Duke Ellington's practice of blending the instruments in endless combinations, producing a whole kaleidoscope of orchestral colour. The musicologist Gunther Schuller wrote: "I don't think there has ever been a master of harmonic modulation in jazz to equal Sauter. His skill in this respect is certainly equal to Richard Strauss's in classical music."[5]

The backings Sauter created for Goodman's singer, Helen Forrest, are among the most exquisite vocal arrangements ever written. But despite the esteem in which he was held by musicians, most of Sauter's career was spent as a jobbing freelance arranger, with occasional forays into composition, mainly for his own satisfaction. His brief career in the public eye came when, in partnership with fellow arranger Bill Finegan (ex-Glenn Miller), he formed and led a remarkable recording and touring band, the Sauter-Finegan Orchestra. In the course of its five-year existence (1952-55) the SFO had several Top 30 hit singles, including 'Doodletown Fifers', 'Midnight Sleighride' and 'Nina Never Knew', and its albums scored sizeable sales figures. The SFO was the first band to employ electronic technology on-stage to reproduce the sounds on their records, with Finegan simultaneously conducting and operating an early form of mixing desk. This meant that very quiet instruments, such as recorders and bass flutes, could be brought forward at appropriate points.

The Sauter-Finegan Orchestra was not a jazz orchestra – although some splendid jazz musicians sometimes played in it – nor a dance band, although it did sometimes play for dancing. The nearest definition would be something like '20th century American light music', but really it defined itself. Back in the mid-1950s, Getz had played a few times on the same concert bill as the SFO. "Eddie invited me to come out and play with the band. I came to a rehearsal and played the vocalist's arrangements with them, and it was just beautiful ... I always remembered it."[6]

The orchestra was vastly expensive to maintain and the costs finally overwhelmed it. Sauter went back to freelance arranging, but Getz's admiration for his talent remained undimmed. He was determined to commission an album of original music by Eddie Sauter, no matter what Verve's new owners might have preferred. "He was writing music for jingles for television programmes," said Getz. "I thought, 'Why should a man this great have to do things like that?' So I asked him to write something for me ... I said, 'I don't want any arrangements on standards, pop songs, jazz classics, or anything. I want it to be all your own original music – something that you really believe in.'"[7]

"Stan is the only one I know who has ever said that and meant it," commented Sauter dryly.[8]

It was decided that Sauter would write a set of pieces for chamber string orchestra, plus harp and percussion, into which Getz would weave his own improvisations. Sauter explained: "I hated the idea of a rhythm section with strings, and I also hated the sound of flat backgrounds with no meaning in themselves ... What I wanted to do was write like a string quartet with space to move things ... let them make their own time and rhythm ... I knew Stan would make it swing.

"I had to do something for Stan, draw something out of him and show him off. I don't like music that shows pure technique or memory ... I wanted to write pieces that had continuity of thought and shape, and had enough thematic strength to hold together, almost in their own right. And I always left, at the back of my mind, a space for another part to be added. I didn't know what was going to happen in that area. That was the hole I left for Stan. That he instinctively found this hole without even knowing it, is a tribute to his sympathy and sensitivity. The way he reacted to the environment of the orchestra was one of the most gratifying things I've ever experienced."[9]

The title of the work was *Focus*. It was scored for first and second violins, violas, cellos, double bass, harp and percussion – 19 players in all, with the Beaux-Arts Quartet acting as its nucleus – and recorded on July 14th and 28th 1961, with Hershy Kay conducting. In fact, only the orchestra was present on the first date, because Goldie Getz, Stan's mother, died of a stroke on the 13th. He spent the seven days of shiva, the period of Jewish ritual mourning, in a drunken stupor, but roused himself in time for the second session. He was now faced with the task of recording the whole work in one day, half of it to a pre-recorded track with headphones clamped on his ears. This would be a difficult enough task in normal circumstances, but he would be attempting something that no-one had ever done before, improvising freely inside a fully composed orchestral work, rather like making up a concerto on the spur of the moment. And it would have to be done in complete takes, the format rendering it virtually impossible to cut and splice the tape. If anything qualifies Stan Getz for the title of genius, it's what he achieved on July 28th 1961.

Focus is, in effect, a suite in seven parts. There is no obvious linking theme, although Sauter did say later that he had conceived the parts as individual stories or fairy tales, "as if Hans Christian Andersen were a musician". Dom Cerulli, who wrote the notes for the original LP release, certainly thought the opening movement, 'I'm Late, I'm Late', called to mind the White Rabbit in *Alice In Wonderland*. It is introduced by a spiky, scurrying theme from the strings, in the middle of which the saxophone appears, apparently hurrying in the opposite direction. The general air of slightly comic haste and confusion is heightened by the addition of brushes on snare drum, played by Roy Haynes. With the mood established, the three-sided conversation continues in the same vein, sometimes at delightfully cross-purposes. Getz obviously grasped the whole idea instantly and jumped with complete confidence into the unfamiliar context. There is no rhythm section, no changes and no beat, in the jazz sense. Instead of the song form in which he had worked all his life, there is simply a free flow of musical ideas. Take away the conventional structures, and the favourite moves that all jazz musicians use to negotiate them will not work – yet Getz still contrives to sound like no-one but himself. His musical vocabulary is so flexible that he can deploy it in any way he chooses.

He recorded two takes of 'I'm Late, I'm Late', both completely different, and when it came to choosing which one to use, Getz, Sauter and producer Creed Taylor simply could not decide. So they used both, end to end, which is why this piece is by far the longest at just over eight minutes. It's followed by the exquisite 'Her', dedicated to the memory of Goldie Getz. The mood is elegiac and the saxophone part more prominent here, although, by contrast with the conventional string 'pad' or 'cushion' effect, Sauter provides the strings with the lightest of textures. In one beautiful passage, Getz's tenor and the solo violin of Gerald Tarack, leader of the Beaux Arts Quartet, curl around one another with such subtlety that it is difficult to believe the two lines were not conceived and composed as a single entity. Because *Focus* is so unlike any previous jazz-soloist-with-strings recording, critics have tended to reach for parallels among the works of various classical composers. The names of Bartok and even Stravinsky have been bandied about in this process. At the risk of adding to these tenuous comparisons, I would suggest that there are moments in 'Her' which have the sparse, ethereal quality of late Debussy.

When Sauter spoke of "leaving a hole" in the music for Getz to fill, one might imagine that the orchestra would take the lead and the saxophone would add a commentary. But this is by no means always the case. In the third movement, a short piece entitled 'Pan', Getz treats the energetic opening string theme as an introduction to his own, even more energetic statement, so that he seems to be leading and the orchestra following him. His tone here is strident, almost raucous at times and, coming immediately after the softness of 'Her', it serves to illustrate the extent to which Getz had broadened his tonal range. The process that began in the mid-1950s with *The Steamer* and *Award Winner,* and continued through his expatriate years, had now brought him to a stage of expressive flexibility commanded by no other saxophonist.

SHARP FOCUS

Although Getz's part in *Focus* is entirely improvised, he did have a written guide in the form of a 'lead-sheet', or short score. In its simplest form a lead-sheet consists simply of the tune with chord symbols attached. In this case it was probably more like an outline sketch of the music, showing the melody line, the general drift of the harmony, some main points in the orchestration, dynamics, and so on. Using this, Getz would have been able to get his bearings, to tell when the orchestration would be dense or sparse, busy or calm, harmonically active or static. His perfect pitch was accompanied by a virtually photographic memory, so one concentrated listening in conjunction with the lead-sheet was probably all he needed in order to fix each piece in his mind and plan his solo.

It is sometimes possible to trace very vaguely how his thought processes worked. For instance, the orchestra opens 'I Remember When', the fourth movement, with what sounds very much like a conventional introduction, before subsiding to a murmur, prompting Getz to enter on a strong, rising, lyrical phrase. Conversely, in the final minute of the piece, the strings play a series of heavy, forceful chords, over which Getz holds long notes. The general principle here seems to be that he moves when the orchestra is still, and remains static when surrounded by energetic activity.

By contrast, the next part, 'Night Rider', is a study in simultaneous movement. Sometimes the saxophone and strings seem almost to be contradicting one another, although Getz always manages to find a resolution. At one point, in an explicit use of the lead-sheet, he plays several bars in exact unison with the first violin. Although it is less than four minutes long, 'Night Rider' amounts to a little masterpiece on its own account, packed with spirit, wit and rhythmic variety.

But the most varied of all is the sixth movement, 'Once Upon A Time'. It tells an entire musical story in the course of its four minutes and 45 seconds, passing from a dark, brooding opening section to a kind of wild country dance. Practically all Getz's experience had been of playing in 4/4 time, because that's what jazz was based on. *Focus* presented him with the challenge of unfamiliar time signatures, which he took in his stride, and in 'Once Upon A Time' he bounces around in 6/8 (or possibly 12/8) as though to the manner born. His rhythmic freedom here is quite remarkable, with phrases cutting blithely across the bar-lines, setting up endlessly diverse patterns of tension and release. The seventh and final part, 'A Summer Afternoon', finds him creating a single, long stream of melody over the strings, mainly in subdued pizzicato, and displaying almost superhuman control of tone.

No jazz musician had even attempted anything like *Focus* before, and very few have ventured successfully into the same territory since (a rare exception is *Memos From Paradise*, a 1988 collaboration between clarinettist Eddie Daniels and composer Roger Kellaway). Getz considered *Focus* his masterpiece, and it's impossible to disagree with him, although it is just as much Eddie Sauter's work as his. They were very fortunate in their timing, too. A few years earlier and Getz's tone would not yet have reached the state of magical luminescence which makes every note he plays on the album so thrilling, and stereo recording would not have been available to capture the subtleties of Sauter's orchestration.

Focus was released in March 1962 and received hugely favourable notices in the music press. Yet in the following year's Grammy Awards it failed to win the prize for 'Best Original Jazz Composition', that award going instead to a piece of impacted kitsch by Vince Guaraldi, called 'Cast Your Fate To The Wind'.

For his last recording sessions of 1961, Getz arranged his long-awaited reunion with Bob Brookmeyer. They were accompanied by Getz's current rhythm section: Steve Kuhn on piano, Roy Haynes on drums, and John Neves replacing the recently deceased Scott LaFaro on bass. Three of the six pieces on the resultant album (titled *Recorded Fall 1961*) are Brookmeyer compositions, full of those clever but unobtrusive little devices with which he habitually sharpened up small band performances, giving them shape and cogency without interfering with their spontaneity. At one point he even a drops in a few choruses backed by a Charleston rhythm. A typical Brookmeyer tune here is the cheery 'Thump, Thump, Thump', which proceeds as a single unfolding melody, without the repetitions customary in popular songs, and inspires exactly the kind of sunny, freewheeling solos that one associates with the Getz-Brookmeyer partnership. They sound as though they have picked up just where they left off at the end of 1954.

The album was released quickly, ahead of *Focus*, in fact. It gained excellent reviews and helped re-establish Getz on the US jazz scene as he toured with the quartet. Coltrane was still topping the polls ahead of him, but his name was once again before the jazz public. Verve Records, meanwhile, were still looking for a formula that would lift him out of the purely jazz category and invest the name of Stan Getz with broad popular appeal. Their ideas seem to have been running along 'easy listening' lines.

In June 1962 they recorded him with a New York studio orchestra, playing the title theme from the hugely popular television series *Dr Kildare*, hoping that this might do the trick. But, unknown to the record company, the trick had already been done. When the single of the 'Theme From Dr Kildare' came out a few weeks later, it was as the B-side to a number entitled 'Desafinado'. The bossa nova had arrived.

CHAPTER 11

The Girl From Ipanema

"I just thought it was pretty music.
I never thought it would be a hit."

STAN GETZ, ON HIS FIRST INVOLVEMENT IN
BRAZILIAN MUSIC, *JAZZ SAMBA*

Jazz had become so popular around the world by the mid-1950s that the US State Department was using it as a propaganda medium in the Cold War. The Voice Of America beamed nightly jazz programmes to the nations of Soviet-ruled eastern Europe, while jazz concert packages toured Third World and 'non-aligned' countries on a regular basis. South America was a favourite destination.

Musicians often brought back records of music that had taken their fancy while on tour, and several came home raving about a new jazz-samba fusion that was beginning to surface in Brazil, its leading figures being the composer Antonio Carlos Jobim and singer-guitarist João Gilberto. A popular souvenir album was Gilberto's *Chega de Saudade*, on the Odeon label. Attempts had often been made to get US record companies interested in this music, but they had met with little success. Capitol released an album by Gilberto in 1960, but it sank without trace.

In December 1961, Getz and the quartet were playing a week at a club in Washington DC. Among their backstage visitors was the guitarist Charlie Byrd, who lived in the city and played there nightly at the

Getz with Astrud Gilberto

Stan Getz NOBODY ELSE BUT ME

Showboat Lounge. Byrd was unusual in that he played both jazz and classical guitar and took a keen interest in many other forms of music. He had recently returned from a State Department tour to Brazil, and invited Getz to come and hear some of the music he had brought home with him.

"Charlie Byrd came into the club one night and asked me if I'd like to stay with him," Getz recalled. "At his place I listened to the João Gilberto LP. He told me about the tour he'd just made for the State Department and about Brazil and all the other countries he'd visited. The idea developed of making an album of some of these tunes."[1]

What was it about this music that so fascinated jazz musicians? In the first place, it inhabited the same harmonic universe as they did. Jobim, Gilberto and co had been listening to modern cool jazz, especially the Gerry Mulligan Quartet and, later, the first Miles Davis-Gil Evans albums. Their melodies and supporting harmonies were constructed along similar lines and seemed to invite gentle exploration. The new samba was not what we should now call 'World Music'. That is, it was never folk music or street music. It was quite unlike the South American styles that had swept the United States and Europe in the past – the tango, rumba, mambo or cha-cha-cha. Like most modern fashions, they had started at the bottom and worked their way up, becoming ever more genteel in the process. But the music that was to become known as 'bossa nova' was reasonably well-bred to start with. If its leading figures – Jobim, Gilberto, Vinicius de Moraes, Luiz Bonfa, Newton Mendonca – had counterparts in north America they would be Mel Tormé, Blossom Dearie, perhaps Mose Allison, or even Cole Porter – sophisticated city artists. The lyricists regarded themselves as poets and the composers regarded themselves as something more serious than simple tunesmiths. The term 'Third World' was just coming into use, but in most people's minds it did not yet apply to Brazil. Brazil was a kind of beach paradise, inhabited by charming, rhythmic people whispering to one another in their attractive, melodious tongue.

"The authentic Negro samba is very primitive," Jobim said. "They use maybe ten percussion instruments and four or five singers. They shout and the music is very hot and wonderful. But bossa nova is cool and contained. It tells the story, trying to be simple and serious and lyrical. João and I felt that Brazilian music had been too much a storm on the sea, and we wanted to calm it down for the recording studio. You could call bossa nova a clean, washed samba, without loss of the momentum. We don't want to lose important things."[2]

Jazz musicians like Getz also took to the bossa nova because they found in it the qualities they saw being lost from jazz. This was certainly how Getz himself felt. As he put it, "The songs of João Gilberto and Antonio Carlos Jobim ... arrived here when anaemia and confusion were becoming noticeable in our music to anyone who knew enough to be concerned."[3] Musicians of Getz's persuasion found in this music melodic themes, subtle harmonic shading, emphasis on a warm tone and intimate delivery. It was almost like coming home.

Getz broached the idea of a jazz-samba record to Creed Taylor, his producer at Verve, who didn't exactly fall over with excitement at the proposal, but thought it might be worth a shot. Getz and Byrd assembled some musicians and tried putting down a few tracks, but they couldn't make it work. Those "clean, washed samba" rhythms proved far trickier than they had bargained for. It was agreed that Byrd would rehearse a rhythm section in Washington DC, made up of musicians who had been with him to Brazil, and call Getz when he judged that they were ready. The call finally came and Getz, together with Creed Taylor, flew to Washington on February 13th 1962. The recording studio turned out to be the hall attached to All Souls Unitarian Church, which Byrd declared to have the best acoustics in the city.

The band he had assembled may have looked slightly odd, but it worked. It consisted of himself on acoustic guitar, his brother, Gene Byrd, doubling bass and guitar, Keter Betts on bass, and two drummers, Bill Reichenbach and Buddy Deppenschmidt. Using two drummers was a brilliant idea. It meant that each could play a simple pattern, the two patterns combining to create a shifting, shimmering beat. They recorded seven numbers in less than three hours. Getz and Taylor packed up and flew straight back to New York, arriving in time for dinner. It had been a productive day, but neither was expecting miracles from it. "I just thought it was pretty music," Getz remarked later. "I never thought it would be a hit."[4]

The album, bearing the title *Jazz Samba*, was released in April. After a fairly slow start, tracks from the album began to be heard on popular daytime radio shows and sales picked up strongly. On September 15th *Jazz Samba* appeared in the *Billboard* pop album chart. By the end of the year it had reached Number Two, and in March 1963 it finally hit Number One – the only instrumental jazz album ever to do so. It spent a total of 70 weeks in the US charts. Meanwhile, a version of 'Desafinado', taken from the album, edited down to three minutes and backed by the aforementioned 'Dr Kildare Theme', entered the pop singles chart in June 1962, where it remained for 16 weeks and reached Number 15 (11 in the UK). If Getz had any doubts about his sudden pop-star status they would have been banished when he found himself appearing as a guest on the *Perry Como Show*. He was also back at the top of the *Down Beat* poll, having narrowly beaten John Coltrane to first place.

THE BOSSA NOVA CRAZE

Jazz Samba remains deeply enjoyable to this day, but when it first came out it was utterly irresistible. Many of us who were around at the time will remember playing it right through, turning the disc over and starting again from the beginning. We couldn't get enough of it and it made us greedy for more. It was as though Getz and these gorgeous Brazilian themes had been waiting for one another, all unawares, and now they were together at last.

'Desafinado' itself, which opens the album, starts with a textbook demonstration of Charlie Byrd's ingenious rhythm section set-up. First, the bass lays down a pattern, based on two alternating chords, the first drummer comes in, simply scrubbing quavers (eighth-notes) with one wire-brush, then the second drummer adds a two-bar pattern, and the whole thing is set ticking like a well-regulated clock. The melody of 'Desafinado' sounds sweet and artless, but not only does it get around some pretty tight harmonic corners, it is no less than 68 bars long, as compared with the 32 of a standard American show tune. Getz's improvised solo is not actually based on these changes at all. The rhythm section reverts to its introductory pattern, alternating just two chords (F and E♭), and he plays over that for 32 bars, before closing with a decorated version of the theme. Structural variety is, in fact, one of the many attractions of this music. Another piece on *Jazz Samba*, the 40-bar 'O Pato', follows the unusual pattern AABCA(i), with many delightful turns along the way.

Jazz Samba made no pretension to be authentic Brazilian music – one only has to glance at the names of those taking part to realise that. It has none of the melancholy that lurks around the edges of even the most sprightly performance by Gilberto or Jobim, but it does contain some devastatingly sharp playing. A case in point is 'Samba Dees Days' (Charlie Byrd's composition, but most likely Getz's title, bearing in mind his lifelong fondness for dreadful puns). This swings ferociously throughout, and the ending has to be heard to be believed. So too does the way Getz sings over Byrd's guitar in 'E Luxo So'. He sounds as though he has known the tune all his life, whereas this was the first time he had encountered it.

The term 'bossa nova' does not appear anywhere on Jazz Samba. It's hard to tell when it was first used, but it was certainly current when Getz's next album, *Big Band Bossa Nova*, came out in October 1962. So what does 'bossa nova' mean? According to Antonio Carlos Jobim, 'bossa' means a lump or bump. In Brazilian Portuguese, to have a 'bump' for something is to have a special gift or flair for it, and 'nova' means new. So, roughly speaking, bossa nova means a new skill or trick.

To write and conduct *Big Band Bossa Nova* Getz chose a 28-year-old arranger, Gary McFarland. McFarland, who was already a bossa nova enthusiast, had been a pupil of Bob Brookmeyer and was widely regarded as a rising star of the studios. The outstanding piece on this album is a version of Jobim's 'Chega de Saudade', incorporating a lively duet passage for Getz and Brookmeyer. The tune itself is a little masterpiece – 68 bars long with no repeats at all. After the first 32 bars in a minor key you think it has reached the end, only for it suddenly to burst out again in the tonic major, heading in the opposite direction. McFarland called it, "One of the best-constructed songs I have ever heard." The 18-piece orchestrations employ no saxophones, using flutes and clarinets instead, and McFarland follows the general pattern set by Gil Evans of using light textures in constantly varying patterns. "I just thought Gary was a great writer," Getz commented. "He knew how to leave space, how to not use every instrument at all times … When you trust a writer you don't want to hamper him by putting in your ideas. He knows what you can do and you believe in him."[5] Sadly, Gary McFarland died in 1971, aged 38, never having quite lived up to his brilliant start.

Big Band Bossa Nova entered the US pop charts just before Christmas 1962 and remained for 23 weeks, reaching Number 13. By now, the field was getting crowded, as bossa nova began showing signs of becoming a major pop craze. In 1961 the record companies had been caught unawares by the sudden eruption of the Twist as a pop-dance fad, and they were determined not to be wrong-footed again. Accordingly the pop industry gobbled up bossa nova in 1963 and spat it out again the following year. During that time everyone from Ella Fitzgerald to the organist at the roller-skating rink was into it, and it didn't stop there. At the height of the craze one could buy bossa nova ballpoint pens, bossa nova gymshoes and bossa nova foldaway plastic raincoats. All this was completely at odds with the subdued art that bossa nova actually was, but nobody worried unduly about that. All you had to do was get the words 'bossa nova' into the song title, stick a few bars of bossa rhythm onto the beginning of the record and you were in with a chance. A classic example was Eydie Gorme's hit single, 'Blame It On The Bossa Nova'. Elvis Presley even tried his hand with 'Bossa Nova Baby'.

When *Big Band Bossa Nova* had been in the shops for about eight weeks, *Down Beat* reported: "Getz now can command a nightly four-figure salary, the royalties from his albums are expected to run ultimately into six figures, and he can count on the kind of lifelong security that only a year ago seemed hopelessly out of reach."[6] No wonder he used to introduce 'Desafinado' (or 'Dis Here Finado', as he had taken to calling it), "the tune that's going to put my children through college."

SAMBA ENCORE!

The bossa nova epidemic raged on, but Getz had so far not had a chance to play with its two greatest figures, Jobim and Gilberto, or even to meet them. Circumstances seemed to conspire against it. In November 1962 a bossa nova concert was staged at Carnegie Hall, sponsored by a magazine, a record company, the Brazilian airline, Varig, and the cultural wing of the Brazilian foreign ministry. With so many fingers in the pie it was bound to result in a shambles, and it did. Getz finally got to meet Jobim and Gilberto, but not to play with them. The Brazilians played two weeks at New York's Village Gate club a little while later, but Getz was on tour and couldn't attend. He eventually had the chance to work with Jobim in February 1963 on his next album, *Jazz Samba Encore!*. Jobim played guitar and piano on some tracks and helped Creed Taylor to set up the sessions, although Getz's main partner was guitarist, singer and composer Luiz Bonfa. This was Getz's first bossa nova recording with Brazilian artists. In addition to Bonfa and Jobim there were two Brazilian percussionists, Paulo Ferreira and Jose Carlos, and, for the first time, a singer – Maria Toledo, Bonfa's blind girlfriend, later to become his wife.

Luiz Floriano Bonfa was as famous in Brazil as Jobim. He composed the bulk of the music for the film *Orpheo Negro [Black Orpheus]*, which in 1960 won the Oscar for Best Foreign Film and the Premier Grand Prix at the Cannes Film Festival. One song in particular from that film, 'Manha de Carnaval', has since become an established standard and is still widely performed today. Bonfa was a virtuoso guitarist and his assertive playing on *Jazz Samba Encore!* elicits a passionate response from Getz. The sound of the tenor saxophone is often compared to that of the human voice, but no player ever uttered a more soaring, songlike timbre than Getz produces here. With its fibrous, airy consistency and broad vibrato it is positively operatic, especially when paired with the clear, pure tones of Maria Toledo. Their performance of Jobim's 'Insensatez' is almost unbearably poignant. It has that quality which Brazilians call saudade, the tinge of melancholy regret, which colours all their music. There is a depth to this first proper collaboration between Getz and authentic Brazilian artists that is absent from the previous two albums, fine pieces of work though they are. Rhythmically, too, it is more subtle. Sometimes the guitars, bass and percussion play so sparsely that the structure is eggshell-thin, but the time is absolutely firm and unshakeable. Bonfa's own 'Um Abraco No Getz (A Tribute To Getz)' drives forward with even greater momentum than 'Samba Dees Days' on the Byrd album, but with half the expenditure of energy on the part of the rhythm section.

Stan Getz NOBODY ELSE BUT ME

Jazz Samba Encore! was undoubtedly the best jazz-and-bossa nova record so far, but it was released onto a market groaning under the weight of bossa nova records and received scant attention, although it did manage a brief spell in the lower reaches of the album charts. *Down Beat* critic John S Wilson put the matter quite candidly. "If this had been one of the early entries in the bossa nova fad, it could have been hailed as something wonderful," he wrote. But he also suggested that "ten years from now it will possibly sound better". The passage of many more years have winnowed out the competition for us now to hear *Jazz Samba Encore!* in its true perspective.

Jazz Samba Encore! was the first in a set of three bossa nova albums planned by Creed Taylor to feature Getz with Brazilian artists. With the benefit of hindsight, we may think he had left it perilously late, but no one could have predicted the magnitude of the craze or the speed with which it would develop. In March 1963, only a couple of weeks after the final session with Bonfa, Getz at last found himself in a recording studio with both Jobim and Gilberto. They had brought with them from Brazil their favourite drummer, the splendidly named Milton Banana. The bassist was Tommy Williams, who had played on the Bonfa sessions. Also present was Gilberto's wife, Astrud, the only member of the party able to speak fluent English.

It is impossible to over-estimate the importance of Jobim and Gilberto to the entire jazz-bossa nova phenomenon. It was Gilberto's Odeon records, brought back from Brazil by Charlie Byrd, which had first captivated Getz and started the whole thing off. Songs written by Jobim and recorded by Gilberto feature on all Getz's bossa nova albums, including his two hit singles, and the overwhelming majority of bossa nova songs which eventually passed into the general jazz repertoire originate with them. It is interesting to compare the versions recorded at the March 1963 sessions with Gilberto's original records. In many cases the vocal part, guitar accompaniment and basic routine are identical, with Getz's saxophone added, rather like *Focus* in miniature. By general consent, the resulting album, entitled simply *Getz/Gilberto*, is the finest work of all in the jazz-bossa nova idiom. Its fragile delicacy, melodic richness and exquisite rhythmic poise place it in a class far above all the others, even Getz's own. It also turned out to be the most popular, and this was partly by accident.

Accounts vary but, at some point during the preliminary rehearsal, someone suggested that it would be a good idea to have a couple of the songs sung in English as well as Portuguese. English lyrics had been put to several of Jobim's songs by now. The 1962 sheet music of 'Desafinado', for instance, bears the title 'Slightly Out Of Tune', with English lyrics credited to Jon Hendricks and Jesse Cavanaugh. This is the version recorded by Ella Fitzgerald, among others. Purely as a demonstration, Astrud Gilberto sang through the English lyrics of 'Garota de Ipanema' ('The Girl From Ipanema'), by Norman Gimbel, and 'Corcovado' ('Quiet Nights') by Gene Lees. Her singing – simple, artless and with slightly wavering intonation – appealed to Getz and Taylor. Why not have Astrud sing the English lyrics? Jobim and João Gilberto were dead against the idea, on the grounds that Astrud was not a professional singer and had never even sung in public before. Their objections were overruled, possibly on the grounds that the record charts were full of singers who should never have been let loose on the public in the first place, and it was agreed that Astrud would sing the English words to both songs.

But the spotlight would, of course, be on Getz's saxophone and the whispering, voluptuous voice of João Gilberto. Every language has its own tune, its own rises and falls and inner rhythms. Languages also have what might be termed individual consistencies – soft or hard, gritty or smooth, sticky or clear. Each country's popular music grows around its language and certain voices seem perfectly matched to its expression. Portuguese, especially the Brazilian variety, is a soft, liquid-sounding language and João Gilberto's sibilant tones drape themselves casually about the words and fall in elegant folds around the melodies of the songs he sings. Miles Davis maintained that Gilberto could sound seductive reading aloud from *The Wall Street Journal*, which just about sums it up.

OUT OF TUNE

The first piece to be recorded, according to the master numbers, bears out Miles's contention. The lyric of 'So Danço Samba' consists mainly of four words: "So danço samba" (I only dance the samba) and "Vai!" (Go!), yet Gilberto manages to make even this harmless message sound vaguely lubricious. After one vocal chorus, it is Getz all the way, over Gilberto's basic guitar pattern, skeletal piano from Jobim, and Williams and Banana playing so quietly that they are only just audible. Yet Getz is able to swing perhaps more ferociously than ever before. Bossa nova is unique among Latin-American idioms in that its rhythm patterns are perfectly compatible with straight-ahead swing phrasing. The first few bars of Getz's second chorus could have come straight out of a late-Thirties big-band swing arrangement, but they sound absolutely right here.

To continue in recording order, the second piece was 'The Girl From Ipanema', of which more anon, and the third the gentle 'Vivo Sohando', in which Gilberto again sings the opening chorus before Getz takes over and plays to the end. The texture of his tone is amazingly rich throughout the whole album. Sometimes the notes are half sound and half air, almost like late Ben Webster, but at the same time full, while his vibrato is broad but minutely controlled. Saxophone vibrato does not come naturally from the chest, like a singer's or flute-player's vibrato, nor is it produced by the fingers, as with a string instrument. Saxophonists make their vibrato by tiny movements of the lower jaw. This varies the pressure on the reed, which is clamped to the lower surface of the mouthpiece. Like everything to do with saxophone tone, vibrato is something that players have to work out for themselves, because the crucial part of the instrument, about two centimetres of mouthpiece, is actually inside the mouth and therefore invisible. Watching Getz play, even quite close-up, provided no clue as to how that extravagant variety of tone was produced. His embouchure (the grip of the mouth on the mouthpiece) appeared completely rigid.

The *Getz/Gilberto* version of 'Desafinado' derives directly from Gilberto's 1958 Odeon recording, on which he was accompanied by a small orchestra arranged and directed by Jobim. Its playing-time was less than two minutes, whereas the one with Getz runs for more than four. The key of the latter is a semitone lower, putting Gilberto at the very bottom of his vocal range and making his voice even more whispery. Getz's solo this time is an elegant elaboration of Jobim's melody and the performance closes with a fade over the two-bar figure which opened the Getz-Byrd recording. By the time this was made, numerous other artists had recorded their versions of 'Desafinado', but none of them came within miles of this meltingly beautiful treatment, nor has it been equalled since.

'Corcovado' opens with Astrud Gilberto singing the opening 16 bars out of tempo, in English. The English lyric, by Gene Lees, is infinitely better than most such efforts, and succeeds in reflecting the nostalgic longing of the original song. Getz, once again, follows the contours of the melody closely throughout his solo. Indeed it is such a beautiful tune, attached to such expressive harmonies, that the lightest of touches does the trick. This song, too, was one of Gilberto's Brazilian Odeon recordings, dating from 1960 – the original now resembles an incomplete sketch, waiting to be filled with the colour and light that Getz eventually brought to it. The piece is also notable for a piano solo by Jobim himself, in his typical minimalist style. Beside Jobim, even Count Basie sounds ornate, but he can be wonderfully effective. His introduction to the next number, Ary Barroso's 'Para Machuchar Meu Coração' sets the mood perfectly and his matching coda brings the piece perfectly to rest.

As we shall see, Getz eventually became heartly sick of playing his bossa nova hits night after night, but one song stayed with him almost to the end, and that was 'O Grande Amor'. It is the longest piece on *Getz/Gilberto* and probably the most deeply felt of all. It's very simple in outline: Getz plays the opening melody, followed by Gilberto, right down at the bottom of his whispering range again, then a piano chorus from Jobim and back to Getz for the last chorus. Nothing spectacular happens, but for sheer delicacy and a palpable sense of musical minds thinking and feeling as one, it is very moving.

GAROTA DE IPANEMA

And so we come to 'The Girl From Ipanema'. For about 12 weeks in the spring and summer of 1964 she was the most famous girl in the world. Her name was Heloísa Eneida Menezes Paes Pinto (later Pinheiro), and all she did was stroll to the beach at Ipanema each morning. Her way took her past a cafe terrace, from which several admiring pairs of male eyes followed her until she disappeared in the crowd. She wasn't to know it but among those admirers were Antonio Carlos Jobim and his friend, the lyricist Vinicius de Moraes. Inspired by the sight of her, they produced a song that was more than just another addition to the girl-watchers' anthology. In its languid melody and easy-going rhythm it summed up perfectly both the physical grace of 17-year-old Heloísa and the rippling charm of the new music that was to become the bossa nova.

This was the song Astrud Gilberto was persuaded to sing in English at the first *Getz/Gilberto* session. Norman Gimbel's English lyric is scarcely a masterpiece, but it does catch the general atmosphere of the original song. What made the record a hit was Astrud's singing. Edited down from almost five-and-a-half minutes to just over three, a pop single version of 'The Girl From Ipanema', consisting of Astrud's vocal and part of Getz's solo, was issued in April 1964. Verve had held *Getz/Gilberto* back for almost a year, partly so as not to interfere with *Jazz Samba*, which was still selling briskly, and partly because the company suspected that the bossa nova craze had peaked.

Monica Getz claimed to have contacted hundreds of disc-jockeys personally, persuading them to listen to the single, and she must have succeeded because it went straight into the charts, and stayed there for some 12 weeks.

Everyone fell for the vulnerable, slightly nervous, impossibly youthful yet sexy sound of Astrud's voice. She was a married woman, but she sounded like an adolescent girl. In one of those magical transfers of identity that sometimes happen in popular song, she turned into the girl she was singing about. She became The Girl From Ipanema. (One of the best-selling paperback novels of that year was *Lolita*, which may or may not be of some marginal relevance.)

Whatever the case, when it finally came out, *Getz/Gilberto* went into the US album charts, reaching Number Two. The only reason it didn't make it to the top was the advent of The Beatles, whose *A Hard Day's Night* hit the US at around the same time. The *Getz/Gilberto* album remained in the chart for 96 weeks, and has never been out of print since. There have not been many times in the history of popular music when the best is also the most popular. There was the swing era, when great instrumentalists like Benny Goodman and Artie Shaw achieved the status of stars. There was the post-war period, when singers such as Sinatra, Peggy Lee, Jo Stafford and Dick Haymes were in the same position. The brief flowering of bossa nova was almost another such period.

Looking back, one of the nice things about bossa nova was the fact that it defied conventional showbusiness wisdom – according to this, songs in foreign languages are box-office poison, unless they have no more than two words and come complete with a new, exotic dance. Even worse poison is instrumental jazz, with no words at all. Yet *Jazz Samba* made it to the top, despite having the dreaded word 'jazz' in the title and no vocals at all. *Getz/Gilberto* has vocals, but mainly in a foreign tongue, and also made it. Finally, there was no bossa nova dance, although several people tried to invent one.

Meanwhile, in March 1963, Getz had one further bossa nova album to record with Brazilian musicians. This time the guitarist was Laurindo Almeida, who had been resident in the US for several years, and had toured extensively as a featured artist with Stan Kenton's orchestra. There were also four Brazilian percussionists, with George Duvivier on bass, plus Steve Kuhn, the pianist with Getz's regular quartet. There is, inevitably, a sense of anti-climax about *Getz/Almeida* after the Gilberto album, although everyone plays very well. During the lunch break on the second day of recording, Getz's saxophone was stolen and he was obliged to finish the day on a borrowed instrument. It wasn't the instrument so much as the loss of the mouthpiece that unsettled him. Trying to play the saxophone with a strange mouthpiece is like wearing someone else's glasses or dentures. It is perhaps just possible to detect a slight thinness in his tone on Almeida's composition 'Do What You Do, Do', the last number recorded on that day, but without knowing the circumstances no-one would suspect anything amiss. *Getz/Almeida* languished on the Verve shelves for more than three years, finally coming out in late 1966, when the bossa nova craze was but a fading memory.

CHAPTER 12

Who Cares?

"I had been playing to impress other musicians, which is very common among young players ... It was through Stan that I discovered who you're really supposed to be playing for. He changed my whole outlook."

VIBRAPHONIST GARY BURTON, WHO PLAYED
WITH GETZ FROM 1964-1966

The bossa nova made Stan Getz's fortune, but the years of its great success were by no means carefree ones for him. When the single of 'Desafinado' won the 1963 Grammy Award for the Best Jazz Solo Performance, and with *Jazz Samba* still figuring in the charts, Charlie Byrd began voicing loud complaints. He pointed out, with more than a little justice, that he had been the instigator of Getz's present success.

He had introduced Getz to bossa nova in the first place, devised the effective format of the *Jazz Samba* band, following their abortive first attempt, chosen the material, assembled the musicians and even picked out a studio. "All Stan had to do," he said in an aggrieved interview with *Down Beat*, "was come in and play."[1] And yet he, Byrd, had received no share of the royalties, nor had his role been acknowledged in the Grammy citation. Creed Taylor replied to that last complaint by pointing out that the prize was for the best solo, and there was no guitar solo on the single, which seems a touch pharisaical, to put it mildly. Byrd finally went to law, securing a lump sum in respect of back royalties and a share in future profits, but

Stan with inspired vibraphone player Gary Burton, mid 1960s

it would not have hurt either Getz or MGM to have done the decent thing and paid up with good grace.

Then there was the question of Getz's continuing mood-swings and violent outbursts. These seem to have been both the cause and the result of his binge drinking. He would become sullen and argumentative, then hit the bottle, then start attacking people and smashing up the furniture, his usual target being Monica. Getz's biographer, Donald L Maggin, consulted a psychiatrist who treated Getz in later life. His opinion was that what Maggin called Getz's "psychic pain" stemmed originally from his mother, Goldie, who was severely depressed herself. Throughout his childhood he had tried to please her, attempting to relieve her depression, but the task had proved impossible, leaving him with profound feelings of failure, remorse and guilt. The violent outbursts represented attempts to break out of this doomed cycle. The drink and drugs may once have provided temporary relief, but now they only made matters worse.

In his book, *Stan Getz: A Life In Jazz*,[2] Maggin provides copious, detailed and harrowing details of Getz's outbursts, based mainly on the testimony of his children and of Monica herself. On many occasions the police were called, and sometimes he had to be arrested for his own safety and that of his family. At least once he attempted suicide by gas. In the light of these events, his extraordinary 1954 letter to *Down Beat* from prison, in which he accuses himself of "degeneracy of mind" appears distressingly consistent. Yet to all outward appearances the family life of the Getzes ran on untroubled in its bustling, harmonious course. Monica became involved with the promotion of his career, even to the extent of occupying an office at Verve's New York headquarters for a while. It's difficult to say how much influence she had over his work, although she obviously felt she did. "Stan has not always been fair to his audience," she said in a *Melody Maker* interview. "I think he respects the people now, though. He tries to show this in the way he does his show and in the songs; the songs are so important ... He's learned that the long, egotistical solos don't necessarily mean anything. They don't particularly communicate."[3] The interview makes great play with the pop success of 'The Girl From Ipanema', comparing its appeal to that of The Beatles.

An effort was certainly afoot to consolidate Getz's position as a pop artist. In October 1963 he recorded the album *Reflections*, accompanied by a string orchestra conducted by Claus Ogerman, with arrangements by Ogerman and Lalo Schifrin. It includes new versions of both 'Early Autumn' and 'Moonlight In Vermont' (Henry Mancini's theme tune from *Charade*, the new movie starring Cary Grant and Audrey Hepburn), and, bizarrely, an Ogerman arrangement of 'Blowin' In The Wind'. Verve were so taken with this last item that they deleted the existing single of 'The Girl From Ipanema' and reissued it with 'Blowin' In The Wind' as the B-side, in place of 'So Danço Samba'. The whole album has a slightly unfocused feeling to it. There is rather too much echo on the tenor and the orchestrations tend to be over-busy. By far the best piece is a good, straight account of 'Spring Can Really Hang You Up The Most', with Kenny Burrell's guitar prominent in the accompaniment.

MONSTER OF A PLAYER

While all these developments were taking place, the Stan Getz Quartet continued as a going concern, playing concerts and clubs. Steve Kuhn left at the end of 1963 and Getz could find no immediate candidate for a replacement. The matter became urgent in January 1964 when the quartet was booked for a three-week tour of Canada, with João Gilberto as guest artist. Getz called his old comrade Lou Levy in Los Angeles for advice. Levy could not think of a pianist who might be up to the job, but mentioned a 21-year-old vibraphone player, Gary Burton, who had recently left George Shearing's quintet and was currently freelancing in New York. (Burton had in fact played in the orchestra on a couple of the *Reflections* sessions.) Whereas all the leading jazz vibraphone soloists used two mallets, one in each hand, to strike the keys, Burton used four, which enabled him to play four-note chords. No one had ever used a tinkling vibraphone as the main chord instrument in a rhythm section before, and the idea intrigued Getz. With the tour looming, he called Burton.

"The first two weeks went terribly," Burton later recalled. "I'd never really done much comping [playing chordal accompaniment to a soloist], and he was real particular about comping. He was used to the best and he hated what I was doing. So I'd try a little bit, and pretty soon he'd get frustrated with what I was doing and tell me to lay out for a chorus or more and let him play alone with bass and drums [Gene Cherico and Joe Hunt]. This went on for a couple of weeks, while I was frantically trying to figure out what to play, when to play, how to stay out of his way. And he didn't know how to tell me. All he could tell me was when he didn't like it. But by the third week things started coming together. I got the hang of how to play with him and he began to like the sound of things."[4]

Burton had been hired for a three-week tour and assumed that their association would end when the tour was over. But Getz asked him to stay on for a further few weeks and he eventually stayed for almost three years. "As I got my own playing together, I began to pay more attention to what he was doing, and discovered this monster of a player," said Burton. "I had no idea that this man was such a major artist. I stood next to him and I would play what seemed to me some incredibly mechanical something-or-other, and he would just play the melody and the crowd would be practically in tears. He played that tenor like he was singing. He had this great ability to communicate with people, and I realised I had been taking the audience for granted. I had been playing to impress other musicians, which is very common in young players. You believe they're your true critics but, frankly, they're not. They're the most fickle and opinionated. They filter everything though their own preoccupations, tastes, preferences and so on. It was through Stan that I discovered who you're really supposed to be playing for. He changed my whole outlook."[5]

A matter of days after returning from Canada, Getz took the quartet into Rudy Van Gelder's studio at Englewood Cliffs, NJ, to record an album for Verve. This was to be a purely jazz production, with no bossa nova within earshot. "Stan wanted to get the group on record, and he was worrying that bossa nova was burying his jazz identity,"[6] Burton recalled. The album, when it came out, was entitled *Nobody Else But Me*, though it had to wait 30 years to see the light of day. The last thing Verve wanted from Stan Getz in 1964 was an all-out jazz album.

The content of the album is obviously based on the programme they evolved during the Canadian tour, and it shows that, in this remarkably short time, Burton had managed not only to work out a way of accompanying Getz effectively, but had begun to contribute new material to the quartet's repertoire. It's also obvious he was already well advanced in the process of creating a whole new persona for the vibraphone in jazz. The most obvious difference lay in his consistent use of four mallets, enabling him to treat the vibraphone almost like an enormous piano. Unlike such distinguished predecessors as Lionel Hampton or Milt Jackson, he rarely if ever turned on the vibrator fans, which create the wavering vibrato from which the instrument gets its name. The resultant sound is clear and crystalline, perfectly suited to Burton's filigree style.

Nobody Else But Me, which was recorded in a single day (March 4th 1964) is a beautiful piece of work. Getz's own playing, especially on the ballads 'Here's That Rainy Day' and 'Little Girl Blue', bears out Burton's observation that he played the tenor saxophone "like he was singing", his voice rising through a vapour of soft vibraphone chords. By contrast, the version of 'What Is This Thing Called Love' rushes along so wildly, at 84 bars a minute, that it has the distinct air of a creature let loose after long confinement. In the two-bar break leading from his theme statement into his solo, Getz plays a rising phrase which takes him to altissimo D, way above the 'official' range of the instrument. Such occurrences are extremely rare in his playing, although it goes without saying that all the 'freak' notes are immaculately in tune.

At first, Burton had not been particularly impressed by the idea of working with Stan Getz. As a sharp young graduate of Boston's Berklee School of Music, he knew little about Getz, beyond the bossa nova and some old records from the 1950s. His first inkling that there was more to the man than he had imagined came when Getz gave him a copy of *Focus*, which impressed him immensely. Burton's composition 'Six-Nix-Quix-Flix' on this album shows the influence of *Focus* very clearly – in its mood, its melodic style and, in particular, its 6/8 time signature. A pretty, fluttering little piece, it is unlike any music Getz had so far played with a small band.

Burton's other contribution is an ingenious arrangement or adaptation of 'I'm Late, I'm Late', aptly titled 'Out Of Focus', cleverly orchestrated (if such a term can apply to a quartet) and full of tonal contrast. In a manner of speaking, Burton also contributed the number entitled 'Sweet Sorrow', written by his friend from Berklee days, Michael Gibbs. Once again Getz's openness to contributions by very young, largely unknown musicians is striking. 'Sweet Sorrow' is a spiky, abstract kind of piece, the kind of thing of which Monica presumably disapproved. She would, however, have loved this treatment of Gershwin's evergreen, 'Summertime', so different from all previous approaches to the tune, with an ostinato bass figure running under it all the way and Getz rising to heights of great passion and intensity. All told, *Nobody Else But Me* marks a high point in Getz's recorded work. It's a shame that the world had to wait until 1994 to enjoy it, especially since Verve did eventually release the results of a session, recorded a few months later, about which Getz was extremely unhappy. This was planned as a quartet album with the pianist Bill Evans, a promising idea on the face of it, but it simply didn't work. Even the best performance, 'My Heart Stood Still', has a rushed, stumbling air about it. Significantly, Getz solos much of the time with just bass and drums accompaniment. For some reason, too, his tone fails to bloom.

Getz/Gilberto was named Album Of The Year in the 1964 Grammy Awards, and 'The Girl From Ipanema' won Best Single. It made commercial sense for Astrud Gilberto to join the New Stan Getz Quartet (as the band was now being billed), to make a profitable touring package. Astrud and João Gilberto had been on the point of separating at the time of the *Getz/Gilberto* sessions, and they were now divorced. Pursuing his usual policy of making a pass at any presentable woman he met, Getz now instigated an affair with Astrud. It was by no means an idyllic relationship. The Girl From Ipanema turned out to be a tough cookie. By all accounts, when they were not either on-stage or in bed, she and Getz spent most of their time together squabbling and fighting. Nevertheless, Astrud and the quartet made an ideal combination and their recordings together have a blithe, insouciant charm that belies the off-stage hostilities.

The album *Getz Au Go-Go*, supposedly recorded live in May 1964 at the eponymous New York club, catches the partnership very well. It later emerged that little, if any, of the original live recordings went into the final version, which was mostly done in the studio, with 'live' effects added. Indeed three of the numbers ('Corcovado', 'Eu E Voce' and 'The Telephone Song') are by a different band altogether, without Burton but including a guitar (allegedly Kenny Burrell) and with occasional touches by a pianist who sounds suspiciously like Jobim himself. Could at least some of these be leftovers from the *Getz/Gilberto* sessions? The whole tangled affair has kept discographers busy for years, but the ease with which performances could be dubbed and spliced by the 1960s makes it unlikely that anyone will ever get to the bottom of it.

Whatever the case, the remaining seven tracks are by the quartet, three of them with Astrud. She sings 'One-Note Samba' in both Portuguese and English, with a wonderfully tricky contrary-motion part by Getz in the middle section of the song. She sounds even younger and more ingenuous in her native language than in English. Also included are two classic American songs transposed into the bossa nova idiom – 'It Might As Well Be Spring' by Rodgers & Hammerstein and Benny Carter's beautiful 'Only Trust Your Heart'. Apart from their undoubted charm, these performances mark a significant step in the incorporation of bossa nova into the jazz vocabulary. It very quickly became common practice occasionally to recast standard songs in the bossa nova idiom in the interests of variety, a practice that continues to this day.

Also included in *Getz Au Go-Go* are further versions of 'Summertime', 'Here's That Rainy Day' and 'Six-Nix-Pix-Clix', together with another Gary Burton original, a perky, quirkish little piece in 12/8 time called 'The Singing Song'. It's obvious from the freedom and relish with which Getz plays on this and other Burton tunes that the young vibraphone player had provided him with a challenge and stimulus in which he delighted.

JUST FRIENDS

Getz's exclusive contract with MGM/Verve allowed him to record, by agreement, as a featured guest with other artists on other labels. It was under this arrangement that he recorded for Columbia on May 25th and 26th 1964, first with Tony Bennett and, on the same day, with Bob Brookmeyer. The rhythm section was the same for both sessions, consisting of Herbie Hancock (piano) and Ron Carter (bass) – both members of the Miles Davis Quintet at the time – and John Coltrane's drummer, Elvin Jones.

The Tony Bennett session yielded only one number, a simple, grave version of 'Danny Boy', to which Getz contributes both obbligato and a restrained solo. Three further numbers – 'Clear Out Of This World',

'Just Friends' and 'Have You Met Miss Jones' – were recorded at a later session, and all four were released as part of Bennett's album *Swingin' Till The Girls Come Home*. Getz often said how much he enjoyed working with singers, and once admitted that he lived in hope of one day being called by Frank Sinatra, "like a bride waiting for the groom."[7] His playing with Tony Bennett suggests that, had it happened, it would have been a memorable meeting.

The remainder of the two Columbia sessions saw Brookmeyer and Burton added to the line-up and resulted in enough material for an entire album, released the following year under the title *Bob Brookmeyer And Friends*. The customary Getz-Brookmeyer magic works again and all eight numbers are superb, from Brookmeyer's jaunty 'Jive Hoot' to Getz's luminous accounts of 'Skylark' and 'Misty'. Getz plays with great drive and intensity on the Gershwin number 'Who Cares?' Once again, he seems to be revelling in the opportunity to play up-tempo swing. One particularly attractive piece is 'Some Time Ago', a jazz waltz by the bassist Sergei Mihanovich, which was in the process of becoming a minor jazz standard. Getz and Brookmeyer share the theme between them and pick up one another's solo ideas in the easy-going way that typified their whole relationship.

The vogue for bossa nova was now winding down, but its connotations of youth, love and freedom were still potent enough for 'The Girl From Ipanema', sung by Astrud with the quartet, to be featured on the soundtrack of the movie *Get Yourself A College Girl*, starring Nancy Sinatra, among others. Perhaps the last great event of the bossa nova years was a concert at Carnegie Hall on October 9th 1964, featuring Getz's quartet with Astrud Gilberto and João Gilberto with his own new band. The bands played a set each, later released by Verve as *Getz/Gilberto 2*, and combined for the final three numbers. For some reason these remained unissued until 1989, when they appeared in a four-CD Verve compilation of Getz's bossa nova work, immaculate to the very last note.

The quartet with Gary Burton was proving to be both stable and immensely popular. It toured widely and wherever it went it drew packed houses and effusive praise from the critics. So it is strange that so little of its music was formally recorded, and even less of it issued at the time. Live recordings were made in concert halls from Canada to Japan, and in Europe there were full-length television programmes, too. The live recording that Verve chose to release was made in November 1966 in Paris, towards the end of the quartet's existence. Gene Cherico and Joe Hunt had departed by this time, Cherico replaced first by Chuck Israels and then by Steve Swallow, and Hunt by Stan's ideal drummer, Roy Haynes.

Despite slightly off-centre balance, the Paris recording justifies all the praise that was being heaped on the quartet. The playing is surprisingly broad, more expansive in gesture than before and almost violent in its sudden changes of mood and dynamics. Getz's ballad feature is a heart-stopping performance of 'When The World Was Young', which comes as close to passionate song as any instrumentalist ever has. Two bossa novas are included among the seven numbers, Getz's personal favourites 'Manha de Carnaval' and 'O Grande Amor', and Burton's 'The Singing Song' receives the workout of its life, with Haynes exploding delightfully in all directions. Burton's own feature is a sweet and completely non-subversive treatment of 'Edelweiss'.

PERIODIC MAYHEM

Apart from touring with the quartet, Getz undertook two major projects in the mid-1960s, both involving further collaboration with Eddie Sauter. The first was the soundtrack music to *Mickey One*, a film directed by Arthur Penn and starring Warren Beatty. Beatty plays the part of Mickey, a nightclub comedian ("I'm a Polak Noel Coward") down on his luck and being pursued by unnamed assailants. We never get to see the pursuers directly, and gradually the possibility dawns that they might be figments of Mickey's paranoid imagination. The sense of unreality is heightened by the fact that few of the characters actually have names; they are 'the Girl' or 'the Agent'. Penn cast Getz's tenor saxophone as a kind of musical doppelgänger to Beatty's Mickey. "What is the sound of terror?" he asked in his notes to the subsequent album of the music. "The sound of loneliness, fear in the city? ... For *Mickey One*, it had to be a sound that would express the central character and reflect his inner life." Getz and Sauter went to great pains to fulfil this brief. During the course of the film Getz can be heard imitating a rock'n'roll saxophonist and a street busker, multi-tracking duets and trios with himself and generally exercising the kind of skills he had not called upon since leaving the NBC staff orchestra.

Mickey One was chosen as the US entry in the 1965 Venice, New York and Rio de Janeiro film festivals, received much critical approval, and flopped miserably at the box office. Arthur Penn and Warren Beatty moved on to make their next movie, *Bonnie And Clyde*, while Getz and Sauter began planning another major work, a concerto for tenor saxophone and symphony orchestra.

Meanwhile, the periodic mayhem which was a permanent feature of the Getz family's domestic life was getting worse, although they were still managing to keep it out of the papers. Monica's *Melody Maker* interview, previously quoted, draws to a heart-warming close as follows: "At home, Stan doesn't practise his horn a great deal. We have five children, you know, and they love to be with him. If he's not doing something special with one of them, he enjoys swimming in our pool and playing ping-pong, or perhaps once in a while entertaining friends."[8]

In December 1965, Getz appeared on-stage at Carnegie Hall with his right foot swathed in bandages, the result of "an accident at home", as it was reported. In a drunken fury, during a fight with Monica, he had smashed his foot through a plate glass door and severed an artery. After one of these outbursts he would be quite calm, even apologetic, but refused to accept that anything was seriously amiss. Yes, he'd admit, he could be short-tempered, but he was under a lot of stress maintaining the almost superhuman standards he set himself. Yes, he loved his wife and children. No, he was not an alcoholic... Monica, on the other hand, believed that drink was the cause of these violent episodes. She had discreetly sought professional advice and learned of a drug called Antabuse, which caused an allergic reaction to alcohol. Getz, asserting that he was not an alcoholic, refused to take it, so she determined to administer Antabuse without his knowledge, and against the guidelines specifically laid down for its use. This decision was to have far-reaching consequences.

The other collaboration with Eddie Sauter, the concerto, was to be part of a major concert at Tanglewood, the outdoor concert arena at Lennox, Massachusetts, which was the summer base of the

Stan Getz NOBODY ELSE BUT ME

Boston Pops Orchestra and their conductor Arthur Fielder. Also contributing music were the composers David Raksin, Alec Wilder and Manny Albam. The Getz quartet, augmented by guitarist Jim Hall, was to be included in some of the orchestrations. The *Tanglewood Concerto* is an ambitious work, and hugely accomplished from all points of view, but it lacks the vital spark that illuminates *Focus*. It is almost as though Sauter, that most judicious of orchestrators, had been overwhelmed by the forces at his disposal. The man whose arrangements for Benny Goodman have been compared favourably with the work of Richard Strauss suddenly becomes diffuse and hesitant.

Getz's first entry, which should have been riveting and memorable, floats by almost unnoticed. As pleasant music for a summer's evening it passes muster, but as a major work the concerto fails lamentably. Far better are Alec Wilder's 'Three Ballads For Stan' and even Albam's brisk recasting of 'The Girl From Ipanema', featuring Roy Haynes. It is said that one piece planned for the evening, Albam's setting of the Jewish lament 'Eli, Eli', did not arrive in time to be rehearsed, much to Getz's chagrin because he had planned it to be the climax of the whole concert.

This story reminds us that, like so many leading figures in 20th century American music, Stan Getz was a characteristically Jewish-American artist, just as Sinatra was characteristically Italian-American, Crosby Irish-American, Bix Beiderbecke German-American, Armstrong and any number of great jazz musicians African-American, and so on. In the case of those from European origins, their American roots were rarely more than two generations deep and fragments of the old cultures still adhered to them, indelibly colouring their music.

Throughout Getz's recorded career, but especially in later life, it's possible to catch a distinctively Hebraic cast in the fall of a note or the sob of an exaggerated vibrato. It was reported that once, on a visit to Israel, he did play 'Eli, Eli', with such feeling that he reduced many in his audience to tears.

CHAPTER 13

Sweet Rain

"I don't hire by age, colour, creed or anything, but these guys are young and their music is young. I hear good musicians, and they happen to be young musicians who want to get out there and play to people."

STAN GETZ, DURING HIS FLIRTATION WITH ELECTRONIC

JAZZ-ROCK IN THE LATE 1970s

Gary Burton left at the end of 1966, with plans to lead his own band. His experience with Getz had provided him with plenty of practice in the more mundane side of bandleading, since he had been the quartet's road manager, in all but name, for the past couple of years. A formidably well-organised person, Burton is often cited by other musicians as the ideal manager, quite apart from his great musical gifts.

The saxophonist Tommy Smith, a member of Burton's band in 1986-7, asserted that no one could get four musicians, plus their instruments and equipment, through an airport and onto an aeroplane more expeditiously than Gary Burton. "He knew how to bypass the crowds, which side-door to use, which guy to tip, and how much to tip him. It was uncanny."[1] Burton went on to a hugely successful international career as a bandleader and soloist, also becoming Dean of Studies at his alma mater, Berklee. His reputation as both musician and academic continues to grow.

Getz disbanded the quartet while he sought a replacement. In the interim, he agreed to help out Verve

Stan in 1974, the year of the Bill Evans reunion concerts

by rescuing a project that had come to grief. The company had planned a ballad album by the guitarist Wes Montgomery, and had even gone to the extent of recording the accompaniments, when renegotiation of Montgomery's contract broke down and he left.

The investment was lavish, consisting of 12 arrangements by Claus Ogerman for an all-star rhythm section, three additional percussion, cymbalom (an east-European zither played with padded hammers), full string orchestra and a large chorus of mixed voices. Equipped with lead-sheets and a set of headphones, Getz supplied the solo 'voice' to all 12 numbers in two sessions. The finished album was named *Voices*. The notes made no mention of Wes Montgomery, but the whole thing is a testimony to Getz's musicianship. To the man who could tackle *Focus* it did not perhaps pose a great challenge, but the tenderness of his playing here is as touching as it is almost anywhere. Some of the pieces actually sound as though they were written especially for him, notably 'Zigeuner Song' and 'Where Flamingos Fly', in which the plangent ringing of the cymbalom contrasts effectively with the saxophone.

For his new quartet, Getz eventually settled on a 26-year-old pianist, Chick Corea, from Chelsea, near Boston, Massachusetts. Corea had previously played with the bands of Mongo Santamaria, Willie Bobo, Herbie Mann and Blue Mitchell. His ideas were developing quickly at this stage and joining Stan Getz, famous for his open-minded attitude to adventurous young musicians, was probably the best move he could have made. "When I joined his band," Corea would recall, "my interest was very much in free music, harder-edged emotions in improvising, longer solos, more disharmonic harmonies, if you can say such a thing. Stan's music was still very lyrical and his renditions were very much to the point. And so one of the jobs I had when I first joined his band was to try to accompany him and play within that format, which actually taught me a lot of much-appreciated discipline. Things like playing a shorter piano solo, and how to accompany him in such a way as to make his lyrical lines sound best. It was very much a learning experience."[2]

Almost immediately, Getz and Corea were in the studio, along with Ron Carter on bass and drummer Grady Tate, and what emerged from those two days' work constituted the next big shift in Getz's stylistic range. The album was entitled *Sweet Rain*, and the first thing everyone noticed about it was the sudden changes in tempo, and even in metre, that occur at several points. Coming from Getz, a master at sustaining a mood, these abrupt switches can be quite disconcerting to begin with. They are tied up, in their turn, with questions of form and harmony. Corea brought with him the interests of his musical generation, which were as radical in their way as those of the beboppers in the 1940s. Albums released in 1967 included Miles Davis's *Nefertiti* and *Sorcerer*, Wayne Shorter's *Schizophrenia*, Joe Henderson's *Tetragon* and Archie Shepp's *One For Trane* – all, in their various ways, reflecting the loosening of form which had followed from the introduction of modal improvisation.

The upheavals of bebop had scarcely affected the traditional chorus form of jazz, being concerned with the elaboration of harmonic changes within the existing chorus structure. But once the very idea of changes, of harmonic resolutions having to take place at certain points, was questioned, then the structure which determined those points was on the way to becoming redundant. We begin to hear fluid or asymmetrical structures. Eventually, there may be no given structure at all other than the tempo, a concept summed up by Miles Davis as "time, no changes". These are the ideas that Chick Corea brought with him to the Stan Getz quartet.

Take, for example, the opening piece, Corea's composition 'Litha'. It alternates between a gentle, reflective section of 30 bars in 6/8 time and a fast 32-bar section in straight 4/4. In former days, the players might well have treated the slow part as an introduction and confined their solos to the second part. This time they improvise on the whole thing, tempo shifts and all. The chords are not 'changes' in the bebop sense. They do not lead or resolve from one to another but drift around almost at random. The fast section has only four chords, each sustained for eight bars (E minor, F minor, A minor and B-flat minor), although these are not so much chords as indications of modal scales. To put it mildly, it's a hell of a long way from 'Long Island Sound', but Getz takes to it as though he has been playing this way for years. In fact, he sounds so at home in the piece that he sometimes jumps onto a tempo change slightly early, as though impatient with the others. Corea's other composition on *Sweet Rain* is 'Windows', a waltz which begins softly and dreamiliy and gradually grows into a passionate, almost savage semi-blues in Getz's treatment. It makes a wonderful study in the way intensity of expression can create a sense of increasing tempo, even when the pulse is as steady as a rock. 'Windows' is also a good example of how a composer like Corea can combine modal and conventional harmonic practice to convincing effect.

'Sweet Rain' itself is a composition by Michael Gibbs, one of several given to Getz by Gary Burton, who later recorded it himself on his album *Duster*. Only ten bars in length, the theme is almost a Getz solo in itself, and the whole performance has a meditative quality about it that contrasts strongly with the vehemence of 'Windows'. The remaining two numbers on *Sweet Rain* are Dizzy Gillespie's 'Con Alma' and 'O Grande Amor', a remnant of the bossa nova repertoire which receives its best and most sinuous instrumental treatment here. 'Con Alma', a standard 32-bar structure, continues the theme of ambiguity by having its main sections in 12/8 and its middle section in 4/4.

COMPLEXITIES

Anyone listening to *Sweet Rain* without having heard Stan Getz for, say, ten years would perhaps not recognise him at first. By 1967, his tone had developed a complexity far beyond the simple, melting beauty displayed in his work with Lou Levy and Leroy Vinnegar. It had become a thing of endlessly shifting colours and textures, of soft crooning disturbed by sudden, forceful interjections, and a vibrato that drifted lazily, like smoke in still air. In the whole history of the tenor saxophone in jazz, no player (not even the phenomenal Ben Webster) ever commanded such a broad tonal palette. From the rising vehemence of 'Windows' to the fragile, sotto voce murmurings of 'Sweet Rain', Getz's manipulation of pure sound is one of the many factors that go to make his first collaboration with Chick Corea the remarkable achievement that it is.

Stan and Monica Getz, whose marriage had begun in a state of bankruptcy, were now rich. With the bossa nova royalties, high-profile projects like *Mickey One* and the Tanglewood concert, together with huge international demand for his personal performances, Getz's annual income in the mid-1960s was estimated at around a quarter of a million dollars. He had achieved the kind of solid affluence that few artists, and virtually no jazz musicians, ever see. For her part, Monica had recently come into a sizeable family inheritance. What was to be done with all this money? The answer was to buy property, a mansion, an estate. It was called Shadowbrook and it stood in nine acres of woods and parkland, overlooking the Hudson River about 15 miles upstream from New York City.

But the palatial surroundings failed to banish whatever demons were tormenting Stan Getz. He had not long been ensconced at Shadowbrook when he went wild towards the end of a small dinner party at home, attacking people and smashing things. The police were called several times and were finally obliged to arrest him. He was let out the next day, by which time his wife and children had fled to the safety of an hotel. Monica obtained a court order decreeing that, should such an incident occur again, her husband would be arrested instantly. This shocked him considerably and he agreed to enter Hazelden, a rehabilitation clinic. It didn't do much good, partly because he kept sneaking out and getting drunk, his accomplice in these escapades being the novelist Truman Capote. Once he was home he soon went back to his old ways. He was duly arrested and the court ordered him back to Hazelden. This time he behaved himself, but began drinking again as soon as he got out.

Between these bouts of violence, arrest and rehabilitation, Getz would go away on tour with the quartet. The trouble always started when he got home. It happened again in August. This time he was committed to a different clinic, Falkirk, where he stayed for ten days and was released on condition he followed a rehabilitation regime and attended therapy sessions, which he ignored. Now, for the first time, Getz's personal tribulations were beginning to affect his playing. Some reviewers found his performance scrappy and unfocused, and he appeared agitated on stage. This was both irritating and frustrating to the members of his touring quartet, who had to put up with it all while trying to play their best. Chick Corea finally decided he had had enough. He left and the band broke up. Not surprisingly, Getz made no records at all in 1968.

Sweet Rain made a big impression on both critics and jazz lovers, demonstrating as it did that Getz had been able to incorporate new developments in jazz successfully into his own playing without in any way compromising his musical personality. Everyone was looking forward to further excursions in this direction but, for the reasons outlined above, it did not happen. Indeed the next two albums to be released both fell firmly into the 'popular ballads with strings' category. These were received with more than their fair share of critical disdain at the time, perhaps because of the marked contrast with *Sweet Rain*. Yet, by all reasonable standards, *What The World Needs Now* and *Didn't We?* are beautiful, expressive, elegantly performed instrumental albums. The former is devoted to the music of Burt Bacharach, by far the most interesting songwriter of the 1960s generation, and certainly the one whose music is most apt for jazz performance. One only has to hear Getz steaming energetically through 'Wives And Lovers' to realise that. Much of the tonal variety of *Sweet Rain* is present, too, notably in the lightly swinging treatment of 'A House Is Not A Home' and the gentle 'Alfie'. It's strange that jazz musicians have not taken to Bacharach's tunes more enthusiastically.

The best moments on the second album, *Didn't We?*, are those where Getz simply lets go with the melody in full operatic mode. He does it in the title song and also in 'Mandy Is Two', where for a few brief moments he sounds uncannily like Johnny Hodges. There is a potentially marvellous swinging version of 'The Night Has A Thousand Eyes', but the echo effect obscures the sharpness of Getz's articulation and the impetus is lost.

TURNING A CORNER

From the personal point of view, things were going from bad to worse. After recording *Didn't We?* in May 1969 he took himself off, alone, to Spain, where he rented an apartment near Malaga. Once there he remained more or less permanently drunk and began to fall seriously apart. He eventually sent for Monica, who arranged for yet another spell in rehabilitation, this time in England. She also began secretly dosing him with Antabuse, the alcohol-allergy drug. After an inconclusive stay at the clinic he returned to Spain and they resumed their up-and-down existence. Throughout 1969 and into 1970 it would have seemed to an outside observer that Stan Getz was in irreversible decline. There are no recordings of any importance, apart from *Didn't We?* and a forgettable concoction, recorded in London, entitled *Marrakesh Express*. According to Maggin's biography, it was treatment for his depression that enabled Getz to turn the corner, to cut down his drinking and take up his career in a purposeful way again.

In June 1970, Stan and Monica Getz travelled to Paris to watch a tennis championship. "As a criminal who always returns to the scene of his crime, I went along to the old Blue Note, where I had played thrice annually from 1959-61," Getz related. "I had been told that jazz in France was dead, and sure enough the club was almost empty. I walked in and my mouth fell open. I heard some hard-core, swinging jazz. Everybody was dipping in, really taking their piece." He had come upon the organist Eddie Louiss, guitarist Rene Thomas and drummer Bernard Lubat. The experience restored his enthusiasm and reawakened his creativity. "I returned to Malaga for the rest of the year, but that foot-tapping music kept repeating in my ears."[3]

He returned to Paris in the autumn and began rehearsing with the Eddie Louiss trio. In December the group appeared for the first time under Getz's leadership at a left-bank jazz club, Le Chat Qui Peche. "As you know, I do not have the reputation for being an indulgent critic, but what happened musically was unique, and suddenly all Paris caught on that something tremendously exciting and new was going on. I decided then and there to present these musicians to the rest of the world."[4] And he did. He toured with them almost until the end of 1971 and recorded a remarkable double album, *Dynasty*.

Eddie Louiss is a most unusual player of the Hammond organ. Almost all jazz organists follow the pattern set down in the 1950s by Jimmy Smith, Shirley Scott and numerous others, namely the funky, rhythm-and-blues-inflected style. It's a simple, straightforward, exciting type of music, irresistibly sexy and danceable at its best, and probably the last form of jazz to command anything like a mass following among African-American audiences. Like the vibraphone and electric guitar mentioned earlier, the Hammond is a 20th century, electro-mechanical invention. Unlike pipe organs and earlier electric types, the Hammond's notes start instantly, with a tiny 'click', and that is what makes it possible to swing on it. Eddie Louiss made a speciality of exploiting the sound of the organ at low dynamic levels, employing subdued washes of sound and varying depths of vibrato. He used the pedals to play the bass part, an accomplishment in itself at some of the tempos Getz liked to choose. Rene Thomas, the Belgian guitarist, was already known to Getz. He had been a member of Sonny Rollins's band in the US. Getz described him as "a gentle soul mixed with absent-minded poetry and earthy gipsy fire". The drummer, Bernard Lubat, had studied percussion at the Paris Conservatoire.

Dynasty was recorded in London, partly at George Martin's Air Studios and partly live at Ronnie Scott's club. Naturally, with this instrumentation, the sound is quite unlike that of any previous Stan Getz record. The compositions are mostly the work of Louiss and Thomas and the majority of tracks are quite long, with expansive solos and slowly building climaxes. Two Louiss numbers, 'Dum! Dum!' and 'Our Kind Of Sabi', are particularly effective in this respect. Each begins with a whispered pattern, the ghost of a jazz-rock groove, and grows into a passionate, full-throated declamation.

The harmonic underlay of these pieces is nothing like as tricky as those devised by Chick Corea. They tend to consist of four or eight bars of one chord, then drop by a tone or rise by a minor third for the next four or eight bars, and so on. But Louiss contrives to suggest so much by his masterly reticence that structure barely enters into it. There is one number, 'Mona', by the German trombonist and composer Albert Mangelsdorf, consisting of almost nine minutes of virtually tempoless recitative, which is absolutely bewitching. The empathy between Getz and Louiss is so close that it comes across as pure feeling.

"The American premise that European jazz musicians cannot swing might have been true in the past," Getz wrote in his notes to *Dynasty*. "The fact is, these guys disproved it." And the swing is indeed prodigious, although in a way unique to this particular band. Rather like the Brazilian bossa nova players, these three contrive to keep everything airborne – sometimes, apparently, by sheer willpower. The number entitled 'Song For Martine' at one point fades away until it is a hairsbreadth from silence, yet the beat is still there. No wonder Getz quotes, elsewhere in the set, from Ellington's 'It Don't Mean A Thing If It Ain't Got That Swing'.

How long the partnership between Getz and Louiss would have continued it's impossible to say. There was still plenty of life left in it towards the end of 1971, when Getz was offered a season at the Rainbow Grill in New York, to begin in January. Unfortunately, the AFM – friend of creative artists everywhere and champion of international goodwill – objected to the granting of work permits to the French musicians, and that was that. Shortly before this, however, Getz and Louiss did feature together on an album composed and conducted by Michel Legrand. Called *Communications '72*, it employed a large orchestra and the vocal group The Swingle Singers. This is one of the least celebrated of all Getz's albums, yet it is packed with excellent playing and fascinating ideas. The title piece, for example, begins with a subdued babble of chattering voices, from which emerge Getz's tenor and a scat-singing voice in unison. The chattering rises and falls in the background as the number progresses, very effectively conveying an impression of hurry and bustle. Other outstanding tracks include a surprisingly funky 'Outhouse Blues', with Getz at his earthiest, and 'Bonjour Tristesse', in which Getz adopts a fragile, almost quavering tone during the quiet opening passage, gradually opening up as the orchestra and voices join in. *Communications '72* is by no means a challenger to *Focus*, but compared with thin, pedestrian stuff like *Marrakesh Express* it indicates that Getz's appetite for trying bold, new concepts was well and truly rekindled.

With his hopes of presenting Louiss, Thomas and Lubat to the American public frustrated, Getz was now in urgent need of a whole new band for the Rainbow Grill engagement. By sheer luck, Chick Corea was between projects and said he would be delighted to organise a rhythm section. He came up with Stanley Clarke, a 20-year-old bassist who was currently causing a sensation among New York's jazz insiders, and the Brazilian percussionist Airto Moreira. After the first rehearsal Getz decided he needed a jazz drummer in addition to Moreira and recruited Tony Williams, formerly of the Miles Davis Quintet. This was the formidable line-up which opened at the Rainbow Grill, atop the RCA Building, on January 3rd 1972. In fact, it seems perhaps a bit too formidable for such a venue, but the management had cannily engaged João Gilberto to share the bill and the show proved to be a sell-out. Getz managed to hang on to the band until the summer, and in March they recorded an album together, *Captain Marvel*.

MARVELLOUS

The history of modern jazz drums in the 1960s can be conveyed in four words: Elvin Jones, Tony Williams. These two between them changed the percussive landscape of jazz, but did it in entirely different ways. Jones created a kind of oceanic roll, amid which the soloist, most importantly John Coltrane, ploughed and bobbed and rose triumphant. His whole style was based on dense textures made up of intermeshing triplets. Williams, on the other hand, would typically start from a strict four beats in the bar, on which, by means of anticipations and subdivisions, he would build a towering edifice of cross-rhythms. Just when it seemed the whole structure was about to collapse under its own weight, he would sweep it away with a nonchalant flick and begin again. Williams had made his debut with Miles Davis at the absurd age of 17, his style already fully formed, and had made a major contribution to Davis's success throughout the 1960s. It was truly said of him that he was a drummer who took no prisoners. Any player who lost his grip on the time with Tony Williams behind him was lost for good.

Stanley Clarke was later to become one of the finest-ever exponents of the bass guitar, but in 1972 he was probably still best known for his double-bass playing. In his hands the instrument could be made to sound like an enormous acoustic guitar. His solos on *Captain Marvel* allow a glimpse of his astonishing virtuosity. At the same time he was a formidable rhythm section player and had been in the bands of both Horace Silver and Joe Henderson. Airto Moreira was a percussion star in Brazil before coming to the US, and had already featured on a number of recent Miles Davis albums.

Captain Marvel, the second Getz-Corea collaboration on record, is quite different from *Sweet Rain*. There is a strong Spanish tinge to Corea's compositions here, and he plays electric piano throughout. This was the first time Getz had worked with any kind of electronic keyboard (the Hammond organ doesn't count), but it would certainly not be the last.

Stan Getz NOBODY ELSE BUT ME

There is a generally turbulent feel to the music, engendered partly by the nature of the pieces, but more by the presence of Tony Williams. The opening piece, 'La Fiesta', grips the attention from the start with its sheer energy. Every corner is filled with movement – busy piano figures, both percussionists hammering away and the bass hopping up and down the flamenco-style chords of the introduction. The melody, when it arrives, is surprisingly simple and catchy, and the solos are based simply on an open modal scale. In this context, Getz approaches the kind of hypnotic frenzy which, in the wake of John Coltrane, was becoming a pervasive mode of address among young saxophonists. With him, it induces a nagging feeling in the listener that he is, perhaps unconsciously, acting a part. He does it so well that to complain seems churlish, but this was the start of a process which led over the next few years to a position in which the music appeared to be playing him, rather than the other way round. As soon as the accompaniment calms down, Getz is his old self again, as in 'Day Waves', a more conventional Latin-American piece by Corea, and a meditative reading of Billy Strayhorn's 'Lush Life'.

Norman Granz, perhaps bored with semi-retirement in Switzerland, was considering launching a new jazz label, to be known as Pablo Records. For its first release, he assembled a 1950s-style JATP company for a concert in Santa Monica. Among those recalled to the colours were Oscar Peterson, Count Basie, Roy Eldridge, Harry 'Sweets' Edison and Stan Getz. As his solo ballad feature Getz chose 'Blue And Sentimental', a sweet old tune indelibly associated with the first Basie band and with Lester Young's friendly tenor saxophone rival, Herschel Evans. The contrast with *Captain Marvel* speaks volumes for the stylistic breadth of which he was now capable.

Chick Corea had plans for a band of his own and left in June 1972 to prepare for it. Stanley Clarke and Airto Moreira joined him later, together with saxophonist Joe Farrell and Airto's wife, Flora Purim. The band they formed, Return To Forever, caught the spirit of the time perfectly and enjoyed great and prolonged success. Getz, meanwhile, found yet another superb young pianist, Richie Beirach and started out again, with Dave Holland on bass and Jeff Williams (later replaced by Jack DeJohnette) on drums. Getz's contract with Verve had come to an end. He was negotiating with Columbia but for the time being he remained in recording limbo. The quartet with Richie Beirach is preserved on a number of live and broadcast recordings. A set from May 1973 at the Famous Ballroom, Maryland, unearthed and issued many years later, contains a particularly gorgeous version of 'Spring Is Here'. Getz plays the not-quite-doubling-tempo game with exemplary cool, and Beirach's comping is exactly the kind he liked in ballads, full-voiced but not distracting. There is also rather good excursion, less hectic than the original, on 'La Fiesta', which had become something of a favourite with Getz's audiences.

One particularly significant event during this interregnum period was a reunion with Bill Evans. Their original effort at making a studio album, ten years before, had turned out to be a disaster, but when they met in Europe in the summer of 1974, everything clicked into place beautifully. Two concerts were recorded by national radio networks, one in Holland on August 9th and the other in Belgium on August 16th, Bill Evans's 45th birthday. The first evening got off to a bad start, with Getz launching right into a tune ('Stan's Blues') that was not on the list they had agreed and rehearsed, whereupon Evans stopped playing and remained silent for the whole number. This minor skirmish aside, both sessions are as close to perfect as an impromptu art like jazz can get. There is no entirely satisfactory explanation why a piece like 'But Beautiful', which sounded so wooden in a New York studio, should assume such tragic grace when played ten years later by the same two principal characters on a concert stage in Antwerp. It is possible that the supporting cast made a difference. In 1964 the bass parts were shared by Richard Davis and Ron Carter, while the drummer was Elvin Jones – certainly not the first name that springs to mind for a job like this. The rhythm section in 1974 was Evans's regular team of Eddie Gomez and Marty Morrell. A tune with the unappetising title 'Funkallero', which had not only defeated the efforts of Getz in 1964 but later those of Zoot Sims too, comes over here as delightfully bright and witty.

Feeling a little remorseful, perhaps, about his gaffe at the previous concert, Getz turned his unaccompanied introduction to 'You And The Night And The Music' on August 16th into an ethereal rendition of 'Happy Birthday', with a touch of 'Always' added. No doubt this went some way towards mollifying Bill Evans, but it also amounts to a remarkable demonstration of instrumental control. There is nothing more certain to show up weaknesses in a saxophonist's sound production than long, unaccompanied notes, especially at extremes of the instrument's range. When it finally arrives, 'You And The Night And The Music' turns out to be the same effective arrangement that Evans devised for his 1962 album *Interplay* with Freddie Hubbard. Getz simply fizzes through his solo, the effervescence leading him to essay one of his rare excursions above the range and into the stratosphere. Altogether the album drawn from these two 1974 concerts, entitled *But Beautiful* and released by Milestone in 1996, contains some of the finest Getz recorded during the whole decade.

INFORMALITIES

The Columbia deal was eventually signed. Judging by early results, most observers concluded that Getz would have done better staying with Verve, even though Creed Taylor had now left and no one else seemed to have much of a clue. Verve now belonged to MGM and, when it comes to jazz, multi-national entertainment corporations never do have a clue. Columbia certainly didn't seem to. Their first attempt was called *Best Of Both Worlds*, and based on the not-very-original idea of teaming Stan Getz with João Gilberto. It features a brassy singer, Heloisa Buarque de Hollanda, whose name is her most impressive feature, a jazz rhythm section plus four Brazilian percussionists, Gilberto and Oscar Castro Neves (who also wrote the arrangements) on guitars, and Getz. His multi-tracked solo on 'Ligia' is curiously attractive, but for the rest of the time he is just an extra, playing obbligatos to the singers.

Matters improved somewhat after that, with a pleasant, although by no means overwhelming quartet album, *The Master*, with Albert Dailey on piano. Dailey and Getz enjoyed considerable musical rapport, and he had toured Europe with the quartet the previous year. The main trouble with *The Master* is that the tracks are far too long for the decent, unambitious nature of the music. The best Getz performance is on 'Lover Man', but the live Belgian version with Bill Evans is better. By far the best, and certainly the most idiosyncratic, of Getz's Columbia albums is *The Peacocks*, which he shares with the pianist Jimmy Rowles

– accompanist to the stars, walking encyclopedia of American song, closet singer and all round good egg. Getz caught his character well in the notes to the album: "Jimmy reminds me of another James – Thurber. His acerbic wit is legendary, but few people know the scope of his skills, ranging from drawing (Thurberish), tennis (Mittyish), singing (indescribably Nat Coleish) and writing (delicious) ... Dammit, I thought, let the world hear Jimmy in a setting he deserves, diamond in the rough as he is, gravelly-loverly voice and all ... I know that Jimmy, the old charmer and grouch, will get all that he deserves – and that's not a second too soon."

The Peacocks has the air of an informal gathering of musical friends. Getz and Rowles play duets, Rowles sings the occasional chorus, Buster Williams and Elvin Jones join in on bass and drums to make up a quartet. For one piece, Wayne Shorter's 'The Chess Players', the singer and lyricist Jon Hendricks, plus his wife and daughter, and Getz's daughter Beverley, add a vocal group. The choice of material is nothing if not original. It includes two fairly out-of-the-way Ellington pieces, 'What Am I Here For?' and 'Serenade To Sweden', Gordon Jenkins's 'This Is All I Ask' and an affectionately jokey rendition of 'Rose Marie'. The sheer fondness with which Getz plays these old melodies is very moving, and Rowles, who in his time had been accompanist to Billie Holiday, Ella Fitzgerald and Peggy Lee, among others, plays throughout with a kind of brusque tenderness which matches it to perfection. In 1977, when the album came out, it was greeted rather coolly, perhaps because the times were not attuned to low-key affairs of this kind. Nowadays it would probably do much better.

When Albert Dailey left the quartet in October 1975, he was replaced by Joanne Brackeen, who moved from Joe Henderson's band. Brackeen was and is an immensely creative musician and this was quite early in a career that burgeoned during the 1980s. Like Chick Corea, she played both acoustic and electric pianos with the quartet. Throughout the 1970s, Getz's regular bands made surprisingly few formal recordings. The best examples of Joanne Brackeen's playing with Getz is to be found in a set of live recordings made in January 1977 at the Montmartre in Copenhagen. They reveal her to be an active and at times challenging accompanist, but Getz clearly relishes the challenge. Occasionally they will push one another to almost unbearable levels of intensity, for instance in the long version of Wayne Shorter's tune 'Lester Left Town'.

EXPERIMENTATION

It's possible to trace the working life of Getz's various quartets by the broadcasts and live recordings listed in his discography.[5] The sheer amount of work and the travelling involved looks quite terrifying. During Joanne Brackeen's first year they touched down, in the following order, at Los Angeles, Hanover (Germany), Hollywood, Ljubljana (Yugoslavia), Kongsburg (Norway), Arhus (Sweden), Copenhagen (Denmark), Rotterdam (Netherlands), New York, and back to Copenhagen again. And these are just the places where they were recorded or broadcast. They also visited Cuba and Israel.

In 1978, Getz told reporter Richard Williams: "For a time I was at a point where I was doing 65 concerts a year." But he preferred playing at clubs. "In a concert you have to lay it on the line once and that's it. In a club people are paying almost to watch you experiment ... The only thing I used not to like about playing clubs was that you had to play three sets a night, which is not civilised. Now all my contracts [specify] two sets a night and I'm happy."[6]

Joanne Brackeen left in July 1977, to be replaced by Andy LaVerne, a 29-year-old Juillard graduate. It was LaVerne who introduced Getz to the world of electronics, most notably the Echoplex. This gadget, an electronic echo-chamber, contained a loop of recording tape which repeated over and over again whatever was played into it. "Imagine," wrote Richard Williams, "two Stan Getzes, then three, then four, six, ten, 20. An orchestra of tenor saxophones played by a battalion of Getzes, pursuing overlapping waves of abstruse but mathematically perfect counterpoint."[7] Nor did it end there. LaVerne added a Moog synthesiser, an Arp string synthesiser and various other contraptions. They could all be heard on *Another World*, Getz's third album for Columbia. The title piece features his Echoplex trick, which is amusing once and becomes screamingly tedious thereafter. Much the same is true of the other electronically enhanced tracks. The few acoustic numbers, especially 'Willow Weep For Me', are fine. The electronics are in evidence, too, on *Children Of The World*, his fourth and final album for Columbia. Arranged and conducted by Lalo Schifrin, it has the distinction of being the most comprehensively panned record of Getz's entire career, and justly so. It contains a version of 'Don't Cry For Me, Argentina' which earns a place alongside 'Dr Kildare' and 'Blowin' In The Wind' in the catalogue of great Getz disasters.

Bob Brookmeyer made a surprise reappearance in February 1978, when he joined up with Getz for a few months. By now the quartet was becoming quite loud and electronic, under Andy LaVerne's influence (Getz was even using a contact microphone on his saxophone in some numbers) and the contrast between this and Brookmeyer's easy, strolling approach made for some awkward moments. There is a particularly good live recording of the band at this time, made in Warsaw, and from this it is clear that it's not so much volume as lack of space that is bothering Brookmeyer. In a number like 'Raven's Wood', by Ralph Towner, the bustling rhythm patterns and busy electric piano crowd in on him so tightly that he has difficulty getting his improvised line started. Getz, being used to it by now, has no such trouble.

In the summer of 1979 Getz took on a 23-year-old guitarist, Chuck Loeb, bringing the regular strength of the band to five. The line-up was now Getz, LaVerne, Loeb, Brian Bromberg on bass, and Victor Lewis on drums. This was the point at which, through the influence of LaVerne and Loeb, Getz travelled furthest from his stylistic base. The classic album by this band is *Live At Midem '80*, recorded in January of that year at the world music business gathering in Cannes. If you drop into it at random you may be forgiven for being a little confused. If Getz is soloing, of course, there will be no mistake about who it is. But if it is LaVerne, or especially Loeb, you might just think you are listening to one of the more musical, pre-punk 1970s rock bands. Loeb's wailing guitar solos, LaVerne's washes of electronic sound, the way Bromberg's bass guitar (another innovation for Getz) doubles the melody beneath Getz, Lewis's drum patterns – all these are directly out of rock music.

Exactly two years earlier, Getz had told Richard Williams, "I've only just got into rock, I'm very new to it. But I'll tell you one thing: I don't think I could take too much of it. The way I feel right now, it's just for once or twice in a set. I couldn't bear to play rock for a whole set, I'd kill myself ... It's too childlike, really

– oom-pah, you know?"[8] A certain amount of 'mission-creep' seems to have taken place over the intervening two years, as he was drawn further into rock territory, willingly or otherwise.

Jazz musicians will tell you that all times are hard times for jazz, but the 1970s were particularly difficult. A large chunk of its previously loyal constituency – students, intelligentsia, the youngish, literate middle class generally – had defected to rock in its various manifestations. And then there was the question of identification. Gary Burton summed it up well when he said, "A roomful of white students see a middle-aged black man in a business suit and they don't identify with him. There's a barrier there, even if he's John Coltrane. With my first band there was no barrier, because we looked like them. We were young, we had long hair and we wore the same kind of clothes. Sounds corny, but it's true."[9] How far such considerations weighed with Getz it's impossible to say. He was adamant that he hired young musicians on merit. "I don't hire by age, colour, creed or anything, but these guys are young and their music is young. I hear good musicians and they just happen to be young musicians who want to get out there and play for people."[10]

On the other hand, he did take subtle steps to distance himself from the 'business suit' image of the middle-aged jazzman. When, at around the time *Captain Marvel* came out, he took part in a Woody Herman reunion concert, Al Cohn and Zoot Sims turned up in their suits, but Getz wore a white outfit with a *Captain Marvel* logo emblazoned across the chest. He was lucky too, in that for a long time he looked younger than his age – which is amazing when you consider the abuse to which he subjected his system.

It's fairly clear that, by the beginning of the 1980s, Getz was beginning to think of stepping back from the front line. His last album with any significant rock influence was made in France in March 1981. It was called *Billy Highstreet Samba*, a play on the name of his Dutch tour manager Billy Hoogstraten. Andy LaVerne had departed, to be replaced by Mitchell Forman, but Loeb was still there, along with bassist Mark Egan (playing what sounds like a fretless bass guitar), Victor Lewis still on drums, and percussionist Bobby Thomas. If it were notable for nothing else, this album would have a place in history for the fact that Getz plays soprano saxophone on two tracks, 'Be There Then' and 'The Dirge'. His soprano sound is not quite a transposition of his tenor, but it is warm, fluffy and light, and floats like a swan over the rippling accompaniment. He had owned a soprano for several years, but had ambivalent feelings about the instrument, perhaps regarding it as rather genteel and lightweight. "It's a Boston instrument if I ever heard one," he said. "A cross between a tin whistle and a flute."[11]

The title tune, Loeb's 'Billy Highstreet Samba', is a gloriously energetic piece, a genuine up-tempo samba rather than a bossa nova, with Lewis and Thomas setting up a terrific barrage at the back. In fact, the rock element is more like Latin-rock throughout, especially 'Tuesday Next', another Loeb composition. But, perhaps significantly, the outstanding track of the album is a feather-light, glancing treatment of a classic ballad, 'Body And Soul'.

CHAPTER 14

Pure Getz

"I'm really not a fuddy-duddy ... I don't think it's a good idea to dote on the past."

STAN GETZ, STILL FORWARD-THINKING

IN THE 1980S

Since recovering from his near-disintegration in 1969, Getz had enjoyed a decade of reasonable stability. Violent incidents still occurred, but they were no longer an ever-present threat. Treatment for his depression had raised the threshold at which the cycle of drinking and violence was set off. He was also being treated, often without his knowledge, with Antabuse. Monica gradually recruited friends, trusted servants, and even some of the children, to administer the drug secretly in food and soft drinks. If he began drinking after taking it he would suffer an allergic reaction.

Experience taught Monica and her helpers just how much Antabuse to employ in order to trigger a mild reaction. It seems he began to believe he was genuinely developing an allergy to alcohol. Nevertheless it was a dangerous practice and medical opinion was firmly opposed to it. Eventually, of course, he found out. A visitor to the house saw what was going on and blurted out the truth. The discovery marked the beginning of the end of his marriage. On the very day when this revelation occurred, January 2nd 1980,

Chet Baker, not Getz's favourite person, joined him for an explosive 1983 tour

Stan Getz NOBODY ELSE BUT ME

Getz and Albert Dailey had been recording an album of duets in the studio at Getz's home. There could not be a greater contrast with the music he was playing nightly with his regular band, and it's tempting to see this album, *Poetry*, as a harbinger of the big change that was soon to come.

Getz admired Dailey, "good old sweet Albert"[1] as he once described him, for his quiet assurance, his modesty, and his sensitive piano playing. Piano and tenor saxophone do not make ideal duet partners, perhaps because the ear is expecting the bass and drums to join in at any minute. There are moments in *Poetry* when this lack is felt, but not many. The ballads, 'A Child Is Born' and 'Spring Can Really Hang You Up The Most', are particularly full and satisfying. This is music of nuance and detail, and as such is quite the opposite of the kind of thing that Getz was playing most of the time – which was music of broad gesture and dramatic effect.

Exactly when he decided to abandon the electronics and general rock-fusion approach is impossible to know. *Billy Highstreet Samba* marks the last recorded appearance of the band of which Chuck Loeb was an influential member. However, Getz had already played a week in January at Keystone Korner, San Francisco, leading a straightforward acoustic quartet with his old comrade Lou Levy on piano, Chip Jackson on bass and Shelly Manne on drums. He joined Levy there again in May, after winding up the electronic band, this time with Monty Budwig on bass and Victor Lewis on drums. After the Keystone Korner engagement, the quartet, with Marc Johnson replacing Budwig, travelled to Europe, playing at jazz festivals and at the Montmartre in Copenhagen.

One night at Keystone Korner was recorded, and later released as two albums, *The Dolphin* and *Spring Is Here*. The latter did not appear until after Getz's death. The material on it had originally been rejected by him as not being good enough, although how he can have come to such a conclusion is a mystery. There is no apparent difference in musical or technical quality between the two.

Anyone picking up a newly released copy of *The Dolphin* in 1981 would have noticed straight away, before hearing a note of music, that Getz had reverted to the type of repertoire – as well as instrumentation – of his earlier career. The six pieces include two American classics, 'My Old Flame' and 'The Night Has A Thousand Eyes'; one jazz theme, Clifford Brown's 'Joy Spring'; two recent songs in the classic mould by Johnny Mandel, 'A Time For Love' and 'Close Enough For Love'; and one Brazilian number, the title piece, Luiz Eca's 'The Dolphin'. But the first playing of the album would soon reveal that this move did not represent a retreat to the safety of playing comfortable old tunes in a comfortable old way. For a vivid illustration, compare 'My Old Flame' here with the light, dandyish version recorded in 1950. Apart from the obvious fact that the later one is more than twice as long, and therefore conceived on a more expansive scale (with a whole chorus from Levy by way of introduction), the 1981 rendition takes a far more inquisitive, almost abstract approach to Coslow & Johnston's song. The harmonies are more adventurous and Getz's playing, while still gloriously clear in outline, is much more ornate.

His tone, by this stage in his life, had reached a level of warmth and flexibility which would have been impossible to foresee in 1950. The tempo is not only slower on 1981, but also much less obvious. In 1950, Percy Heath plays metronomic four-in-a-bar bass throughout, immaculately placed and perfectly in tune, but very basic, and matched precisely by Don Lamond's brush strokes. In 1981, the basic beat is clearly still there, but more subtly stated. During the course of the evening captured on *The Dolphin* and *Spring Is Here*, Getz revisited several more songs from his earlier repertoire, including 'How About You' and 'You're Blasé', both from *The Steamer*, his 1956 album with Levy, and roughly the same observations apply to these.

'Joy Spring' has one of the most elegant chord sequences in jazz, but also one of the most challenging. The merry little tune wriggles its way through some fiendish key changes in the course of its 32 bars, and to follow Getz as he negotiates them is a constant source of delight. The nimbleness of his mind is quite amazing in situations like this, and this is precisely the quality he had little scope to exercise in the rock context. Perhaps it is hindsight which imbues this performance with an air of relief and emancipation.

The Dolphin was released by Concord Records, a company firmly in the tradition of enthusiast-run labels stretching back into the late 1930s. It had been founded in 1972 by Carl Jefferson, a strong-minded individualist whose growing catalogue reflected his own conservative but discriminating taste in jazz. Because he had made a considerable fortune in the motor trade, Jefferson's business was largely self-financed and he was answerable to no one but himself. After his recent difficulties with Columbia, Getz was only too happy to do business with Carl Jefferson.

GET CURRENT

Looking back on the 1970s, his period with Columbia Records and the whole electronic period, Getz certainly tended to dwell on the negative aspects of the experience. "There was a good deal of pressure to keep up to date. The favourite phrase was 'get current'," he recalled. "So I hired some good young electric musicians and tried it. Now, they're electric and I'm acoustic, just a microphone, so I said, 'Just balance around me.' But every night their confidence grew, and as it grew they played louder and I got more uncomfortable. It really felt alien to me. After all, I've spent my life trying to make acoustic sounds. It got so bad that I even tried using a contact microphone. Have you ever wondered what it would be like trying to play the saxophone in boxing gloves? Well, that's how it was. I just didn't feel I was in charge of the instrument. So in the end I got tired and disgusted with being current, and I decided I wasn't going to listen to helpful advice from record company executives ever again. And you know what? I felt better right away."[2]

He was keen, however, to dispel any notion that he might be interested in playing the nostalgia card. "I'm really not a fuddy-duddy or a mouldy fig. I don't much like listening to my own records, because whenever I do I think I could have done better. The guy who's writing my discography sent me a whole pile of tapes, hours and hours, but to tell you the truth, I got bored. I don't think it's a good idea to dote on the past."[3]

Getz had by now left Shadowbrook, the marital home, and was based in San Francisco. It was here that most of his next studio album, *Pure Getz* was recorded, in January 1982. The quartet now had a new pianist, Jim McNeely, formerly of the Thad Jones-Mel Lewis Orchestra. McNeely, who held a Bachelor of

Stan Getz NOBODY ELSE BUT ME

Music degree from the University of Illinois, followed the pattern of his predecessors by contributing new material – both his own compositions and pieces he thought might take Getz's fancy. One of the latter was 'Blood Count', the last composition of Billy Strayhorn, Duke Ellington's collaborator for almost 30 years. He wrote it for an Ellington Carnegie Hall concert a few weeks before his death in 1967 and the Ellington orchestra, featuring the great alto saxophonist Johnny Hodges, recorded it shortly afterwards. It is an achingly poignant piece, and Hodges's playing of it carried such a wealth of feeling, and bore so many fond associations, that his came to be regarded as the definitive version. When Hodges died in 1970, 'Blood Count' was looked upon almost as his personal property. Getz had not even heard it until Jim McNeely brought it to him. He read the lead sheet through once and recorded it straight away, in one take. It turned out to be one of the finest single pieces among his recorded work. Getz's ability to grasp the essence of a piece instantly has been remarked on before, but his rendition of 'Blood Count' goes beyond exceptional musical intelligence. There is something almost supernatural in the way he shapes the phrases and turns them to catch the light.

Pure Getz is a classic album. Apart from 'Blood Count', it contains a formidable excursion on the 12-bar blues, in the shape of 'Sippin' At Bells', written in 1947 by the young Miles Davis for his first session as leader, and an exquisite piece in waltz-time by Bill Evans, entitled 'Very Early'. McNeely's own composition, 'On The Up And Up', shares many characteristics with the music Getz had been playing with his electric bands – boiling Latin rhythm patterns, modal-type harmonies, a lot of activity going on behind the saxophone solo – but the acoustic nature of the music means that everything remains in its natural perspective, as anyone who heard this band playing live will confirm. The number was featured at every concert during the quartet's brief European tour in April 1982.

Once again, enough material was later found left over from the *Pure Getz* sessions for another whole CD. It was issued by Concord, under the title *Blue Skies*, in 1995. Among its contents is a glorious, seven-minute rendition of 'Spring Is Here', perhaps the most affecting of the Rodgers & Hart ballads. There are some songs that forever bear the imprint of a single great recording, and it's impossible nowadays to listen to 'Spring Is Here' without the echo of Sinatra's impassioned interpretation in the background. Perhaps only Getz could have devised an instrumental parallel to Sinatra's version, conveying the same sense of bleakness and loss. Similarly, McNeely creates a setting which enhances the mood, and a solo which sustains it, as effectively as Nelson Riddle's arrangement for Sinatra. Indeed the partnership between Getz and McNeely reached its peak with their ballads. *Blue Skies* also contains a meltingly beautiful account of Gershwin's 'How Long Has This Been Going On?'

As the years passed, the shadows cast by jazz history gradually lengthened. Reunions starring the surviving members of classic bands were becoming increasingly popular items at jazz festivals, along with 'tributes' to great figures who were no longer around. Even a dedicated anti-nostalgic like Stan Getz could not remain aloof from a reunion of the Four Brothers saxophone section, or a tribute to Lester Young, or JATP-style jam session with such figures as Harry 'Sweets' Edison, Gerry Mulligan and Lionel Hampton. He may have had some misgivings when he learned that all three events were to take place on the same day,

June 30th 1982, at the Kool Jazz Festival in New York, but he made it to them all. The first two were included in the 'official' festival recordings issued soon afterwards, and the Four Brothers set, in particular, is excellent. The four in question are Getz, Zoot Sims, Al Cohn and Jimmy Giuffre. Although their tones and styles had diverged considerably since their days with Woody Herman, they were able to drop right back into the old format and create a perfect blend.

GET CURRENT

Getz continued with his sporadic attempts to give up drinking, but sooner or later some upset or crisis would cause him to fall off the wagon. He now had a new companion, Jane Walsh, herself a former alcoholic, and she made great efforts to help him stick to the various sobriety regimes he tried to adopt. As far as he was concerned, his marriage to Monica was over, but Monica strongly resisted all suggestion of a divorce. Furthermore, Jack Whittemore, his business manager, on whom he had relied for many years, died suddenly in January 1983. Both these factors put him under additional strain. This was the precarious state of affairs when he set off for a 35-date tour to Holland, Denmark, Sweden, France and Saudi Arabia in February, on which the quartet was to be joined by Chet Baker. Jane Walsh arranged with Wim Wigt, the Dutch concert agent who set up the tour, that Getz and Baker should travel separately, stay in separate hotels and spend as little time in one another's company as possible. Apart from their mutual animosity, the presence of Baker and his notorious heroin habit spelt constant danger.

Chet Baker was not quite the washed-up has-been portrayed by common gossip among jazz insiders. His health was frail, and there was always the possibility that he might not turn up, but, despite having lost all his teeth, he could play like an angel on a good night. His singing, little more than a whisper now, had a candid simplicity that disarmed critics. Above all, there lingered about him an ineffable glamour, a last remnant of the Golden Boy aura of 30 years before, when it had looked as though he might become, as one commentator put it, "James Dean, Frank Sinatra and Bix Beiderbecke, all rolled into one."[4]

Things went badly from the start. "Stan Getz was like a spoilt child, and he was very insecure," recalled Wigt. "He was jealous of the success that Chet was enjoying. So there was constant conflict."[5] Jim McNeely observed, "Stan had a real attitude about Chet's using drugs. Perhaps if they had been doing the same substance they might have got on better together."[6] The format for the concerts was that Baker would play a set with the rhythm section, Getz would play the second set, and the two would come together for a few numbers at the end. From this point, Getz tended to treat the event like a contest or trial of strength, pulling out the stops, playing with a vigour that Baker could clearly not hope to match. "It was tough on Chet, who, as anyone who knew him would tell you, was really a sweetheart," said Wigt. "Everybody loved him and enjoyed his music ... But because of Stan's inflexible attitude, there wasn't the kind of interplay I hoped for ... The two of them were in different zones and there was no real empathy."[7]

The two Stockholm concerts, on February 18th, were recorded and eventually released as a triple-CD set. They reveal that, despite personality clashes and backstage dramas, some really inspired music was played that night, even when the two antagonists were together on the stage. Both versions of 'Sippin' At

Bells' are full of ideas and rhythmic spirit, and Baker certainly does not sound in the least intimidated. Even the brief passages of simultaneous improvisation come off well. From the second concert comes a version of 'Dear Old Stockholm', which, naturally enough, draws a round applause after the first few notes. Far from crowding him out, Getz hands virtually all the solo space to Baker.

Getz himself performs with the almost nonchalant grace that marks all his best work. There is a further version of 'Blood Count', almost equal to the studio original, a turbulent 'On The Up And Up', and 'O Grande Amor', taken at an unusually fast tempo – almost three hours of music in total, all of the highest, most concentrated quality. The degree of sheer mental and physical energy required, especially from McNeely, Lewis and bassist George Mraz, is something to contemplate. Add to this the fact that they had to do it nightly for a month, not to mention the travelling involved, and the achievement becomes even more remarkable.

The final explosion came during the visit to Saudi Arabia, where they were to play for a Western cultural society in Jeddah. For a Jewish alcoholic it was scarcely the most welcoming of prospects, and Getz was already in a highly nervous state. Baker had contrived to sneak a supply of heroin into the country and proceeded to fall asleep at the US ambassador's dinner table. Getz refused to continue unless Baker left, and Wim Wigt had no option but to drop Baker from the remainder of the tour. The two would not meet again. Chet Baker died in May 1988, after falling from a window of an Amsterdam hotel.

THE GUEST STAR

The Stockholm concerts, which had yielded such splendid and unexpected results, were originally recorded for broadcast by Sweden's national radio corporation. From now on, the vast majority of Getz's quartet releases would come from this and similar sources. In fact, it is worth bearing in mind that a large proportion of the music from Getz's great final burst of creativity, from 1983 until his death, would not have been preserved had it not been for the existence of European public broadcasting networks and the European Broadcasting Union, which arranges for the reciprocal exchange of material among its members. The technical quality achieved is as good as any studio recording, and better than many.

The practice of including star instrumentalists on records by popular singers, as a kind of exotic condiment, became widespread in the later 1970s and continues to this day. To have the words 'Guest soloist: Stan Getz' on an album sleeve was a valuable bonus, although he was sparing with such appearances. Tony Bennett, Julio Iglesias, Cybill Shepherd, Kim Basinger, The Manhattan Transfer, even Huey Lewis & The News – they all benefited from his presence. Sometimes, as with Tony Bennett, it was more than just a token appearance. Sometimes, as on Cybill Shepherd's album *Mad About The Boy*, he sounds as though he is thinking about something else most of the time. In his later years, though, he undertook a few quite serious collaborations with vocalists, none more so than his involvement with the blind singer and pianist Diane Schuur.

He first encountered her in 1979, when, at Dizzy Gillespie's invitation, she sat in on a set at the Monterey Jazz Festival and caused a minor sensation. Getz, whose snap musical judgments were rarely wrong, promised to do whatever he could to help her. He mentioned her name to promoters and club owners, but nothing much came of it until, in 1982, a few prominent jazz musicians were asked to introduce protégés at an event held at the White House, aimed at bringing young performers to public notice. Getz sponsored Diane Schuur, and this resulted in her being signed to GRP Records, albeit via a management deal with a company Getz had set up for the purpose. He played on Schuur's first three albums, *Deedles* (1984), *Schuur Thing* (1985) and *Timeless* (1988), which established her reputation. Her fulsome and emotional style may be something of an acquired taste, but there is no denying her musicality. Her phrasing and intonation are impeccable, and she is able to command an easy, unforced swing.

By the mid-1980s there was always an air of occasion about a Stan Getz appearance. He had attained the stature of an international concert artist, and his name was known well beyond the jazz world. He could, had he wished, have coasted downhill on his fame, relying on well-loved tunes, his seductive tone and the fond associations his name aroused in several generations of listeners. Needless to say, he did nothing of the sort.

CHAPTER 15

Voyage

> *"They used to record Duke Ellington's band*
> *just the way it was that night – first take*
> *and that was it. I like it that way, because*
> *the music changes every night."*

STAN GETZ, PLEASED WITH THE URGENCY AND
PASSION OF HIS 1987 TOUR RECORDINGS

Since moving to San Francisco, following the breach with Monica, Getz had gradually become drawn into the musical life of Stanford University, which was "five minutes drive or 20 minutes by bicycle"[1] from his home in the suburb of Menlo Park. He played benefit concerts, took part in workshops and seemed to enjoy being treated as an artist rather than as a star or celebrity. He was touchingly aware of his own educational shortcomings, and demurred from any suggestion that he should assume a formal teaching role. Instead, at the beginning of 1986, he was appointed artist-in-residence.

"Jazz is on the curriculum now," he said at the time, "and that's something which was unthinkable when I was starting out. Jazz musicians have always been forced to live a gipsy life, in some pretty bad environments, getting no respect at all. It's America's music, but America is only just getting around to recognising it. I'm just doing my small part in changing things.

"At first I was nervous about it. I had no formal background, no matriculation, just 40-odd years in the

Stan on-stage in Nice, 1987, before returning home for major surgery

college of hard knocks. But then I heard how Elizabeth Bishop taught poetry at Yale. She didn't have a syllabus of work, or exercises in – what do you call them – iambic pentameters. She simply read poetry with the students and conveyed understanding that way. So that's what I do. We play together and talk about points as they come up. I think it works quite well and it's very satisfying."[2]

By all accounts, talented students found his participation useful and even inspiring, but he could not communicate well with the earnest plodders. This is hardly surprising. Getz, with his perfect pitch, his photographic memory, his immense natural facility, and a tone that apparently came direct from God, was the last person to think himself into the mind of a keen but not particularly talented 19-year-old. By his own admission, he had only the haziest idea himself of how he did what he did, apart from a vague theory about the 'alpha state'. One recalls Gary Burton's comment about his own induction into the Getz quartet: "He didn't know how to tell me. All he could tell me was that he didn't like it."

Getz declared that he tried to instil originality in students, and encouraged them to "play what they feel". He also said he disapproved of learning by imitating one's heroes.[3] This is strange, bearing in mind his own early days. One wonders what he might have said to a student who had the temerity to bring up the subject of Kai's Krazy Kats, in which he had so assiduously played the part of Lester Young, or the session of July 31st 1946, when he was clearly under the spell of Dexter Gordon. Perhaps fortunately, no argumentative and historically-minded students seem to have presented themselves. As for playing what one feels, what possible meaning can such a dictum have for a young person struggling with the mechanics of music? During the conversation with Getz quoted above, which took place backstage at London's Royal Festival Hall, the author was casting about for some way of delicately broaching these matters, when a gaggle of visitors arrived and the talk turned to the comparative merits of various breeds of dog, which was probably just as well.

At the time of his induction as artist-in-residence at Stanford, Getz's public performances had become irregular, and he had done no significant recording for two years. The upheavals in his personal life, his repeated attempts to overcome his alcoholism, the prolonged and bitter divorce proceedings, in which Monica was fighting tooth and nail to prevent a final break – these had all but derailed his professional life. But the arrangement with Stanford called upon him to give a number of concerts per year, and this seemed like the ideal moment to begin again. James McNeely was now busy with other projects, so Getz invited Kenny Barron to join himself, George Mraz and Victor Lewis to make up a new quartet. Their first appearance was at Getz's inaugural Stanford concert in March 1986, and a few days later, at a studio just off the campus, they recorded Getz's first formal album in four years. It was entitled *Voyage*.

It's clear from the first minute or so that Getz had once again found a pianist to provide the challenge on which he thrived. Even among the higher echelons of advanced jazz piano, Barron's imaginative fluency was, and is, remarkable. Born in 1943, he started as a teenage prodigy in his native Detroit and was a member of Dizzy Gillespie's quintet before the age of 20. In 1986, when he joined Getz, he was already combining a busy performing schedule with a teaching post at Rutgers University. One of the qualities that must have appealed strongly to Getz was his harmonic ingenuity, an ability to find interesting new paths through even the most familiar chord sequences. Nowadays, treatises and instruction books on jazz harmony include quotations from Barron's work more frequently than from almost any other source. There are 25 instances in Mark Levine's *Jazz Theory Book* alone. To follow his delicate elaboration on the simple chords of 'I Thought About You', the second piece on the *Voyage* album, is a typically absorbing and delightful experience.

Getz's own playing throughout *Voyage* is easily on a par with *Pure Getz*. His solo on 'Yesterdays', in particular, amounts to a small masterpiece of consistency and sustained development. His opening theme statement contains several triplet figures, an idea which is picked up by Mraz, who plays the first solo. When Getz enters for his own solo, accompanied only by Mraz, he continues to elaborate on the triplet idea until there is a suggestion of 12/8 about the whole performance. Then, at the beginning of the fifth chorus, Barron and Lewis enter and the feeling of 12/8 gives way to a vigorous, striding four-in-a-bar, with Getz giving vent to a whole series of those passionate, wailing cries that came increasingly to characterise his later style. Finally, after a total of eight choruses, the solo draws to a close with a further string of triplets as he hands over to Barron, who catches them and begins building his solo at that point.

The whole piece, including a sustained closing duet-cadenza for Getz and Mraz, runs for just under nine-and-a-half minutes and is an impressive display of the jazz art at its most accomplished and sophisticated. After listening to it, one can see why Getz felt the jazz quartet was his ideal setting. "In a quartet, I'm able to phrase differently every night. I'm up there and I can freely do whatever I wish to do ... It's essentially a classical-jazz approach to music."[4]

Quite apart from its artistic merits, *Voyage* represented a great personal achievement for Getz. It was the first time he had recorded without the aid of drink or drugs of any kind. The fact that he was able to bring it off at all proved that his efforts to beat his alcoholism had finally been successful. He never took drugs or alcohol again.

URGENCY

On the evidence of various informal live recordings, Getz's playing blossomed in the months following the *Voyage* session. Typical of these is a recording made at a concert in Santa Cruz on March 6th 1987 in which he hurtles through a ten-minute version of Victor Feldman's 'Seven Steps To Heaven' with all the fluid velocity of the celebrated 'Shine', but with a new urgency and force.

From all points of view, it is an astonishing performance, but there is every reason to believe it was not exceptional for Getz at this period. Interestingly enough, it seems that he still felt obliged to play brief court to 'The Girl From Ipanema' during his American concerts, although she had long ceased to make appearances in Europe. The Santa Cruz performance features the tune alongside 'Desafinado' in a brief, not to say perfunctory, medley.

It was around this time that Getz began the practice of playing at least one ballad a night (usually Billy Strayhorn's 'Lush Life') without any amplification at all. He would either have the sound system turned off or simply push the microphone away. As a demonstration of projection, as opposed to mere volume, it was impressive. The sound would carry to the back of the average concert hall with very little loss of clarity. His reason for doing this, he said, was to show that music was essentially an acoustic art and that amplification should be its servant, not its master. "One night when I had the amplification turned off, a young boy came up to me afterwards and asked what kind of sound system I was using. He had never heard natural acoustic music in his life – didn't believe you could make music without all that stuff."[5]

The musical partnership between Getz and Kenny Barron continued to flourish. The quartet's European tour in July 1987 (with Rufus Reid replacing Mraz) was rapturously received, and its performance at the Montmartre, Copenhagen, by now almost a second home to Getz, resulted in some of his finest later recorded work. Danish radio recorded the performance of 6th July for broadcast. Getz acquired rights to the tapes and compiled an album of what he considered the best numbers. It was issued on the Emarcy label, under the title *Anniversary*. Five further long pieces came out in 1991, on a CD called *Serenity*. The abiding impression is one of simplicity and clarity, moderate tempos for the most part, and every phrase crisply enunciated. To anyone able to follow music, to grasp the shape of an unfolding line and respond to the nuances of tone, Getz speaks here with a kind of sincerity, an almost desperate urgency. It's as though he wants you to hear what he hears in these rhythms and moving harmonies. This may be a fanciful notion, in which case the reader should ignore it, but the sheer intensity of expression, not to mention the almost telepathic sympathy between Getz and Barron, is unmistakable.

To take a few examples from this session almost at random: listen to the second and third choruses of his solo on 'Stan's Blues', in which he manages to suggest the essence of the blues with a few cries and bent notes, a twisted quotation from 'Lazybones' and a fleeting half-reference to Charlie Parker, all in the space of 24 bars. In 'I Thought About You' (totally different from the Voyage version, incidentally) the closeness between Getz and Barron makes it impossible to tell who is leading whom through this constantly changing harmonic landscape. In 'I Love You', one of the few up-tempo pieces (at about 64 bars a minute), Getz plays hide-and-seek with the time, placing phrases across the barlines in a most adventurous and masterly way. And this version of the now almost obligatory 'Blood Count' is perhaps the best and most poignant of the many he recorded during these final years. Getz was certainly happy with the results of the Montmartre session, and with this method of recording. "So many records come out now that are products. This is more like the old way. They used to record Duke Ellington's band just the way it was that night – first take and that was it. I like it that way, because the music changes every night."[6]

Several commentators remarked on the urgency and vehemence of Getz's playing during the 1987 European tour. He had always put everything into his performances, but during that summer there was an added passion to them. He would sometimes bang the saxophone keys down so violently that the instrument visibly shook, and the high, throaty, sobbing cries which had lately come to feature strongly in his style now resounded with even greater intensity. It was not generally known at the time that Getz was, in fact, suffering from cancer and faced major surgery on his return to the US. There was a likelihood he might not survive. With hindsight, the new fervour in his playing may perhaps be interpreted as a kind of rage. He had finally rid himself of his old, self-destructive habits only to be faced by this new threat.

The operation, to remove a tumour from behind his heart, was indeed serious. The procedure took eight hours. It was successful but left him in a very debilitated condition. There was also the problem of dealing with the inevitable re-addiction to morphine, but even this was finally overcome and Getz gradually recovered. Afterwards, like the Fat Boy in *The Pickwick Papers*, he took delight in making his listeners' flesh creep as he recounted the gory details of his operation: "They couldn't get in there with what they call a skinny-needle biopsy to see if it was malignant or not, so they just went in to get it. They cut me open like a chicken... Went through the ribs, broke some ribs, collapsed a lung and got it out."[7]

Clearly, playing the saxophone would be out of the question for some time – but, to everyone's surprise, he announced that he was planning yet another European tour for February 1988. It turned out not to be a good idea. He opened in Amsterdam, played a few more dates on the continent, followed by one in London, and was then forced to throw in the towel. "The lungs worked fine, everything worked fine, but it was just a matter of stamina, I guess. I came out too soon. I thought I was going to rough it, push ahead, but now I'm not feeling too good."[8]

Roughing it and pushing ahead was his usual way of dealing with obstacles. His strength of will was quite astounding. Only a few days before abandoning the tour, when he was already showing clear signs of exhaustion, he told the author, "I'll make it. I'm a Russian Jew, and we're the most stubborn people in the world." In support of this assertion, he then proudly recounted his grandfather's odyssey from Russia, via London, to the US. The human quality he admired most, he said, was grit. It is not widely recognised that Getz made a hobby of collecting books, pictures, newspaper cuttings and memorabilia concerning heroes. During that brief, fraught visit to London he still found the energy to ask for a copy of *The Times'* obituary of Robert Stanford Tuck, the Battle of Britain fighter pilot, who had recently died.

TRIUMPH

Apart from some isolated concert performances and a few appearances as featured guest on other people's albums, Getz passed the remainder of 1988 and the first half of 1989 in recuperation. Although the operation had been successful, it was discovered that he now had cancer in his liver. This much-abused organ was already in a pretty bad way, and the prognosis was not good. He was given no more than a year to live. However, the disease went into remission and Getz declared that he felt fine. Eventually, in June, he felt ready to tackle a full European tour.

Before it began in earnest he recorded six numbers in Paris with the singer Helen Merrill. This was a much more serious undertaking than the average guest spot. Helen Merrill was an artist with hugely impressive credentials: she had worked exclusively in jazz since joining Earl Hines's band in 1952, at the age of 21, and her recording partners to date had included Clifford Brown, John Lewis and Stephane

Grappelli. Like Getz, Merrill has a gift for expanding and elaborating a melody without losing touch with its original shape and essence. When he plays obbligato to her voice, the two lines dovetail to perfection, while his solos are wonders of melodic insight. From both points of view, their version of 'Cavatina' must rank high among the countless interpretations of this much-worn piece. Getz sails through 'It Don't Mean A Thing', at around 74 bars a minute, employing half the number of notes that anyone else would have used, but deploying them with such ingenuity that there is a surprise at every turn. The rhythm section of Joachim Kuhn, Jean-Francois Jenny-Clark and Daniel Humair sounds determined not to give him an easy ride, which is plainly how he likes it. Unfortunately, a second session to complete the album never took place. It was eventually issued by Emarcy under the title *Just Friends*, with three unrelated tracks added to fill up the space.

The tour itself took in eight countries, and recordings, both official and unofficial, attest to the fact that it was a triumph. Getz had now adopted a regular format for his concerts. He opened each half with a classic standard, which might vary from night to night, and followed with a fixed programme of Kenny Barron originals, Gillespie's 'Con Alma', Benny Carter's 'People Time', Mal Waldron's 'Soul Eyes', Thad Jones's 'Yours And Mine' and the now-mandatory 'Blood Count'. The first thing to be said is that none of this sounds like the work of a dying man. In fact, he had rarely sounded in better spirits. The veteran American critic Ira Gitler, holidaying in Italy, caught the concert in Perugia and was clearly taken aback by the vitality of Getz's "long and enthralling" concert. It was, he declared, "the kind of night on which the audience would have sat there as long as he continued playing".[9]

The most complete memento of the 1989 tour is the recording made at the Glasgow Jazz Festival by BBC Radio Three and subsequently released on the Concord label. The band consists of Kenny Barron, Ray Drummond and drummer Ben Riley, replacing Victor Lewis. The set-openers are both Cole Porter songs, 'You'd Be So Nice To Come Home To' and 'What Is This Thing Called Love?'. Their opening choruses alone could serve as a model of how to play the melody virtually straight and at the same time make it sound utterly personal. There is a feeling of animation here, even in the slowest of ballads, which lifts the entire performance. One senses it particularly in the lovely 'People Time', written by Benny Carter to celebrate the bicentenary of the USA. Getz played this piece so often that he must have felt special affection for it, and he plays it here with enormous relish. He holds notes as long as possible, conveying the full texture and grain of his tone, and his rhythmic poise at such a slow tempo is impeccable.

WALTZ FOR STAN

The assured mastery of his playing during the 1989 tour was reflected in his fit appearance and confident manner on stage. The contrast with the Getz of 16 months earlier struck everyone as verging on the miraculous. When he returned home and attended hospital for a check-up, it was discovered that the cancer in his liver had receded greatly. The news encouraged him to take up an offer made to him the previous year by Herb Alpert, the popular trumpeter, composer and general music business operator. Alpert, whose first fortune had been made from novelty records such as 'The Lonely Bull' and 'Spanish

Flea' with his band, the Tijuana Brass, was about to become a multi-millionaire from the sale of A&M Records, in which he owned a half share. His admiration for Getz was genuine and long-standing. He proposed an album featuring Getz in an orchestral setting, partly formally composed and partly along the lines of *Focus*, with the saxophone left completely free to improvise. The principal composer was Eddie Del Barrio, an associate of Alpert's, although the credits on the final product read: "All songs written by Eddie Del Barrio, Herb Alpert and Stan Getz."

The CD, entitled *Apasionado*, is by no means a successor to *Focus*, but neither is it the slice of unmitigated kitsch which some critics have accused it of being. It belongs with the Bacharach and *Didn't We* albums as craftsmanlike popular music of a high order. Its only serious failing is an excess of mock-Spanish flummery in some parts. Getz's own performance is quite exquisite. His tone never sounded more seductive than it does on the title piece and Del Barrio's 'Waltz For Stan'.

Apasionado was recorded with an orchestra of 14 players. It sounds much bigger because two synthesisers take the place of strings in creating washes of background colour. When Getz took the music on tour, in the summer of 1990, there was no orchestra, but the synthesisers, played by Del Barrio and Frank Zottoli, did an effective job of recreation. However, it received a fairly cool critical reception – which was sad, since this turned out to be Getz's last tour. Towards the end of the year the cancer in his liver returned and he began to go rapidly downhill. In February 1991 he recorded an album, *You Gotta Pay The Band*, with the singer Abbey Lincoln, the session pictures from which reveal him as gaunt and drooping. He plays as inventively as ever, and matches Lincoln exquisitely, but the phrases in his solos tend to be shorter than usual.

Plans had been made for Getz and Kenny Barron to fly to Copenhagen to play a series of duet sessions for Danmarks Radio at the Montmartre. Following his principle of "roughing it and pushing ahead", he succeeded in playing four complete sessions, which is remarkable when you consider that the duet, with no bass and drums to lean back on, is a particularly testing form. The double CD, *People Time*, taken from these sessions is the very last Stan Getz record of all. As a document of spirit and determination against the odds, it is impressive. Coming from almost any other tenor saxophonist it would have been counted a creditable effort, but it is not how Stan Getz would have wanted to be remembered.

He died at Malibu on June 6th 1991. He had given instructions that his body was to be cremated and his ashes scattered at sea. The melancholy task of carrying this out fell to Getz's boyhood friend Shorty Rogers, whose boat was to be used for the ceremony: "We went out about six miles. It was a very calm day, early in the morning, no wind. We decided this was the place and slowed the boat down. Herb Alpert had brought a CD player and he started playing some of Stan's music. Everyone came up to the forward part of the boat and for about 20 minutes not a word was spoken, just the music floating out over the water. We scattered the ashes, everyone threw a rose onto the water. Still nobody spoke, just a few tears. Then we turned about and sailed back to the shore."[10]

CHAPTER 1: ANOTHER TIME, ANOTHER PLACE,
  pages 8-13
1 Martin Williams *A Jazz Panorama* (Crowell-Collier
  1962).
2 Hentoff/Shapiro *Hear Me Talkin' To Ya* (Dover 1955).

CHAPTER 2: A TUXEDO AND A TOOTHBRUSH,
  pages 14-21
1 Interview for BBC Radio Two (1999).
2 Unpublished interview with Ann Duggan,
  Barbados (c1973).
3 Unpublished interview with Ann Duggan,
  Barbados (c1973).
4 *Scientific American* November 1st 1999.
5 Unpublished interview with Ann Duggan,
  Barbados (c1973).
6 Unpublished interview with Ann Duggan,
  Barbados (c1973).

CHAPTER 3: KAI'S KRAZY KATS, pages 22-29
1 Sheila Tracey *Bands, Booze & Broads*
  (Mainstream 1996).
2 Radio announcer, AFRS December 6th 1944.
3 Unpublished interview with Ann Duggan,
  Barbados (c 1973).
4 Max Jones *Talking Jazz* (Macmillan 1988).
5 Howard Lucraft *Crescendo* 1990.
6 Max Jones *Talking Jazz* (Macmillan 1988).
7 Ross Firestone *Swing, Swing, Swing* (Norton
  1993)

CHAPTER 4: FOUR BROTHERS, pages 30-39
1 George T Simon *The Big Bands* (Collier 1967)
2 Conversation with author, 1991.
3 *Down Beat* July 1990.
4 Conversation with author, 1992.
5 Ira Gitler *Swing To Bop* (OUP 1985).
6 *Metronome* December 1946.
7 *Metronome* September 1947.
8 Conversation with author, 1992.
9 Conversation with author, 1977.
10 Lou Levy quoted in Gene Lees *Leader Of The
  Band: The Life Of Woody Herman* (OUP 1995).
11 Gene Lees *Leader Of The Band: The Life Of
  Woody Herman* (OUP 1995).
12 Lou Levy quoted in Gene Lees *Leader Of The
  Band: The Life Of Woody Herman* (OUP 1995).

13 Scott DeVeaux *The Birth Of Bebop* (University
  of California Press 1997)
14 *Down Beat* May 1966.

CHAPTER 5: LONG ISLAND SOUND,
  pages 40-51
1 Ira Gitler, notes to *Prestige* album P-24088.
2 Unpublished interview with Ann Duggan,
  Barbados (c 1973).
3 *Metronome Year-Book* 1950.
4 Conversation with author, 1989.
5 Quoted by Alun Morgan in notes to *Stan Getz:
  Roost Sessions* (Vogue VJD 573, 1981).
6 *Metronome* December 1950.
7 Note to *Lee Konitz In Sweden* 1951/53 (Dragon
  DRLP 18, 1979).

CHAPTER 6: MOVE, pages 52-61
1 Bill Crow, notes to *Complete Recordings Of The
  Stan Getz Quintet* (Mosaic MD3 –131).
2 *Jazziz* August 1990.
3 *Down Beat* May 1952.
4 *Down Beat* May 1966.
5 *Jazz Journal* June 1994.
6 Notes to CD *Stan Getz: West Coast Jazz* (Verve
  557 549-2).
7 Conversation with author, 1999.

CHAPTER 7: EVERYTHING HAPPENS TO ME,
  pages 62-71
1 *Los Angeles Herald-Express* December 19th
  1953.
2 *Seattle Post-Intelligencer* February 13th 1954.
3 *Los Angeles Times* February 18th 1954.
4 *Down Beat* April 21st 1954.
5 Interview with Steve Voce, BBC Radio
  Merseyside, 2000.

CHAPTER 8: GHOST OF A CHANCE, pages 72-81
1 *Down Beat* May 19th 1966.
2 Quoted in notes to *Award Winner* (Verve 543
  320-2).
3 Quoted in notes to *West Coast Jazz* (Verve 557
  549-2).
4 Max Jones *Talking Jazz* (Macmillan 1988).
5 Quoted in notes to *Award Winner* (Verve 543
  320-2).

CHAPTER 9: FINE AND DANDY, pages 98-107

1 Conversation with author, 1986.
2 *Down Beat* April 14th 1960.
3 Told to the author by the bassist, who did not wish to be identified.
4 Gunther Schuller *The Swing Era* (OUP 1989).

CHAPTER 10: FOCUS, pages 108-117

1 *Down Beat* February 28th 1963.
2 *Down Beat* February 28th 1963.
3 *Down Beat* June 8th 1961.
4 *Down Beat* May 19th 1966.
5 Gunther Schuller *The Swing Era* (OUP 1989).
6 Quoted in notes to *Focus* (Verve 821 982-2).
7 *Crescendo* March 1989.
8 Quoted in notes to *Focus*.
9 Quoted in notes to *Focus*.

CHAPTER 11: THE GIRL FROM IPANEMA, pages 118-127

1 *Down Beat* March 28th 1963.
2 Quoted in notes to *Antonio Carlos Jobim* (Verve 516 409-2).
3 Notes to LP release of *Getz/Gilberto* (Verve V6-8545).
4 *Down Beat* March 28th 1963.
5 Quoted in notes to *The Bossa Nova Years* (Verve 823 611-2).
6 *Down Beat* March 28th 1963.

CHAPTER 12: WHO CARES?, pages 128-137

1 *Down Beat* August 29th 1963.
2 Donald L Maggin *Stan Getz: A Life In Jazz* (Morrow, 1996).
3 *Melody Maker* August 1st 1964.
4 Conversation with author December 18th 1993.
5 Conversation with author December 18th 1993.
6 Notes to *Nobody Else But Me* (Verve 521 660-2).
7 In conversation with journalist Stan Britt, 1983.
8 *Melody Maker* August 1st 1964.

CHAPTER 13: SWEET RAIN, pages 138-151

1 Conversation with author, 1995.
2 Interviewed for BBC Radio Three.
3 Note to *Dynasty* album (Verve 2657 009).
4 Note to *Dynasty* album (Verve 2657 009).

5 Arne Astrup *New Revised Stan Getz Discography* (Soeborg 1991).
6 *Down Beat* January 12th 1978.
7 *Down Beat* January 12th 1978.
8 *Down Beat* January 12th 1978.
9 Conversation with author, 1986.
10 *Down Beat* January 12th 1978.
11 Max Jones *Talking Jazz* (Macmillan 1988)

CHAPTER 14: PURE GETZ, pages 152-159

1 Notes to *Poetry (*Elektra Musician 60370-1).
2 Conversation with author, part published in *The Observer* February 21st 1988.
3 Conversation with author, part published in *The Observer* February 21st 1988.
4 Brian Case *The Hip* (Faber 1986).
5 Quoted in notes to *Getz/Baker, The Stockholm Concerts* (Verve 537 555-2).
6 Quoted in notes to *Getz/Baker, The Stockholm Concerts* (Verve 537 555-2).
7 Quoted in notes to *Getz/Baker, The Stockholm Concerts* (Verve 537 555-2).

CHAPTER 15: VOYAGE, pages 160-167

1 Conversation with author, part published in *The Observer* February 21st 1988.
2 Conversation with author, part published in *The Observer* February 21st 1988.
3 Conversation with author, part published in *The Observer* February 21st 1988.
4 Quoted in notes to *Voyage* (Blackhawk BKH 51101).
5 Conversation with author, part published in *The Observer* February 21st 1988.
6 Interview with Keith Howell, LBC Radio, London, February 1988.
7 Interview with Keith Howell, LBC Radio, London, February 1988.
8 Interview with Keith Howell, LBC Radio, London, February 1988.
9 *Jazz Express* August 1989.
10 BBC Radio Three July 1991.

Song titles are in 'Single Quotes'. Albums etc are *In Italics*. Page numbers in **bold** indicate illustrations.

Stan Getz NOBODY ELSE BUT ME

PHOTOGRAPHIC CREDITS

The pictures reproduced in this book came from a number of sources, as detailed in this list organised by page number. The publishers would like to thank Peter Symes for finding the material, as well as all the photographers, agencies and archives who helped with this endeavour. LP and CD covers came from the collections of Stan Britt, Dave Gelly, Peter Symes, and Joop Visser.

Jacket front: Ray Avery Jazz Archives. **Jacket inside**: Frank Driggs Collection. **1**: Stan's axe, Tim Motion. **3**: Lee Tanner. **9**: Frank Driggs Collection. **15**: Frank Driggs Collection. **23**: Frank Driggs Collection. **31**: Ray Avery Jazz Archives. **41**: Lee Tanner. **53**: Ray Avery Jazz Archives. **63**: Robert W Parent. **73**: Frank Driggs Collection. **82-83**: Apollo and Teagarden shots, Frank Driggs Collection. **84-85**: Herman saxes, Popsie Randolph (Frank Driggs Collection); Goodman, Clayton etc, Bob Willoughby (Redfern's); with Raney, Robert W Parent. **86-87**: hayrick, Lars Hansen; Johannsson etc, Christen Hansen; Down Beat, Ray Avery Jazz Archives; Johnson, Lee Tanner; Getz & Johnnsson, Randi Hultin; with Gourley, Duncan Schiedt Collection. **88-89**: with case, Ray Avery Jazz Archives; Stan profile, Robert W Parent; Haynes, Lee Tanner; Stan with trio, Lee Tanner; with Goodman etc, Robert W Parent. **90-91**: Israels etc, Val Wilmer; Byrd, Lee Tanner; with Astrud, Val Wilmer. **92-93**: Hall, Val Wilmer; UK group, Jan Persson; with Chet, Lee Tanner; hand on face, Jan Persson. **94-95**: cheeks, Jan Persson; with Remler, Tim Motion; profile, Jan Persson; Williams, Lee Tanner; with Mulligan, Jan Persson. **96-97**: Lewis, Jan Persson; Stan sitting, Tim Motion; Stan in shadows, Peter Symes. **99**: Terry Cryer. **109**: Ray Avery Jazz Archives. **119**: Lee Tanner. **129**: Lee Tanner. **139**: Jan Persson. **153**: Per Husby. **161**: Tim Motion.

AUTHOR'S ACKNOWLEDGEMENTS

Two books have been my companions throughout the task:

Stan Getz – A Life In Jazz, by Donald L Maggin, proved most useful in providing a chronological thread and instructive in its copious details of Getz's personal life.

The New Revised Stan Getz Discography, by Arne Astrup, is a work of formidable scholarship, and has guided my musical explorations.

My warmest thanks go to my friends and colleagues Steve Voce, Keith Howell, Chris Howes and Stan Britt for generously providing me with music and interview material, and to Peter Symes for his wide-ranging picture research. Britain's National Jazz Archive, under its amiable and tireless administrator David Nathan, has proved invaluable, yet again.

I met and spoke with Stan Getz on several occasions and found him both courteous and obliging.

This book is dedicated to the memory of Spike Robinson, tenor saxophonist, friend and complete gentleman.

"As I got my own playing together, I began to pay more attention to what he was doing, and discovered this monster of a player. I had no idea this man was such a major artist."
Gary Burton in 1993 on his time with Getz, 1964-66